A WELL-TRAINED TONGUE

TONGUE

Formation in the Ministry of Reader

The Lord GOD has given me a well-trained tongue,
That I may know how to speak to the weary
a word that will rouse them.

Isaiah 50:4

Acknowledgments

The scripture quotations contained herein are
adapted from the *New Revised Standard Version of
the Bible*, copyright © 1989 by the Division of
Christian Education of the National Council of the
Churches of Christ in the United States of America,
and are used by permission. All rights reserved.

The lectionary texts contained herein are adapted
from the *Lectionary of the Canadian Conference
of Catholic Bishops,* copyright © Concacan Inc.,
1992, and are used by permission of the copyright
owner. All rights reserved.

The NRSV, approved for liturgical use in Canada,
is used throughout *a Well-Trained Tongue* because of
its particular suitability for public proclamation.

Editor: Martin F. Connell
Production editor: Deborah Bogaert
Design and cover art: M. Urgo
Production artist: Jim Mellody-Pizzato
The illustration on page 8 is by Shayne Davidson
This book was typeset in Cheltenham, Fenice
and Palatino and printed by Bawden Printing Inc. of
Eldridge, Iowa.

Library of Congress Cataloging-in-Publications Data
Rosser, Aelred R. (Aelred Robert)
   A well-trained tongue: formation in the ministry of
reader/Aelred R. Rosser.
     p. cm.
    1. Lay readers — Catholic Church — Handbooks,
manuals, etc. 2. Catholic Church — Liturgy —
Handbooks, manuals, etc. 3. Lectionaries —
Handbooks, manuals, etc. I. Title.
BX1915.R66 1996
264'.02034 — dc20   96-8689
                        CIP

ISBN 1-56854-124-4
WTTNEW

A WELL-TRAINED TONGUE

Formation in the Ministry of Reader

Aelred R. Rosser

Liturgy Training Publications

Contents

1 *The Minister and the Word*

When you answer the call to be a minister of the word (one who proclaims the Bible readings to the assembled faith community), you enter a deeper relationship with the word of God as revealed in sacred scripture. You take upon yourself the duty and privilege of bringing the printed word to life — making it flesh, so to speak. Your ministry as reader gives voice to God's healing and strengthening word as it goes forth irrevocably to the ends of the earth, achieving the purpose for which God sent it. In a very real sense, you become a prophet — one who speaks for God. You become another John the Baptist preparing the way of the Lord, making crooked paths straight and rough places plain. You take upon yourself the task and joy of delving ever deeper into the mystery of God's presence in the world through the revealed word. You join yourself to an ancient tradition in Jewish life that sees no more worthy occupation than the study and service of God as experienced in the sacred texts. As a Christian you identify yourself with the age-old belief that God's words find their fullest expression in one perfect word: the word made flesh, Jesus the Christ.

As you begin this new ministry, or as you seek to enhance a ministry which you have performed for quite some time, recall frequently that the degree and kind of relationship you establish with the word is the wellspring of your service. As the relationship deepens, you will see yourself more and more as a disciple — one who is not merely taught but *formed* by the Master. And it is precisely as a well-formed disciple that you will be most effective in revealing the face of the Master to those whom you are called to serve.

The minister

The reader proclaims the word to the assembled faith community. It's that simple and that sublime. It is a simple ministry, but not in the sense that it is easy to do well or can be done with little energy or effort.

Simplicity refers to the mode of this ministry, the reader's ability to proclaim the word transparently so that the word itself — not the proclaimer — is placed in the foreground. Simplicity does not refer to the reader's task, either, for the task itself is quite challenging. Not everyone is equal to it.

There is an element of the sublime in the work of the reader as well. To be chosen to proclaim God's word to fellow believers is to participate in the mystery and struggle of their individual journeys in faith. No ministry can be more sublime, and no responsibility more humbling — for the quality of the reader's proclamation determines whether his or her service will help or hinder the hearers.

Men and women who take on the ministry of reader are presumed to be of good faith, eager to serve their fellow Christians and willing to engage in ongoing formation into effective service. But it is not presumed that they are particularly holy, exceptionally gifted or highly skilled in communication techniques. Basic abilities are required, and these are the subject of part of this book. Highly developed communication skills related to certain professions (public speaking, broadcasting, acting, for example) must be developed by the reader, but they do not in themselves render a person capable of effective liturgical proclamation. The purpose of liturgical worship is very different from the purposes we find in the work of professional communicators to convey information, entertain, persuade to action and so forth. The liturgy may do all of these things, of course, but they are not its purpose; its purpose is to celebrate the faith shared by the worshipers.

Finally, the mere wish or willingness to serve as reader does not qualify one for the ministry. This statement sounds harsh; no one wants to discourage a volunteer. But the fact remains that the ministry of reader is a charism for the building up of the community. It requires certain native abilities that some do not have, such as an adequate vocal instrument, for example. It also requires self-possession, confidence, maturity, poise and sensitivity to the diversity in one's audience. Such qualities can be enhanced in a formation program but should be present to a significant degree already in the potential reader.

Like all official ministries in the church, liturgical proclamation of the word is an awesome responsibility to which a person is called and into which one is formed. Fifteen hundred years ago, St. Benedict wrote in his *Rule:* "They should not presume to read who by mere chance take up the book. . . . Only those are to discharge these duties who can do so to the edification of the hearers."

The word

When we hear the expression "the word of God," we think of far more than a simple "word." The "word" of God means "all the words of God." To some it means "the Bible." To Christians it means "the word made flesh," the "incarnate word." The familiar liturgical dialogue that follows every reading — "The word of the Lord"/"Thanks be to God" — has a formative influence on us over time. It creates in our hearts and minds an association between the words of the reading and the benevolent actions of the God who revealed them.

That association is even more vivid in the languages in which the texts we hold sacred were originally written. The Hebrew word for "word" is "dabar," which means "deed" (an action) as well as "word." By this definition, words are not merely sounds or symbols that describe deeds but are *themselves* deeds. Our tendency at this point might be to see such an association as merely poetic. But "word as deed" is not an understanding found only in the highly intuitive thought characteristic of the Middle East, where our scriptures were born. Language scholars in the contemporary West have formulated a similar view. They have demonstrated that words are not always just sounds or written symbols that *refer* to something, as in "There is the house I live in." In some usages, words actually *do* something, and in these cases they are called "performative speech acts." A simple example: The words "I baptize you," or "I forgive you," or "Bless you!" do not simply refer to actions; they actually accomplish the actions they describe.

The point is that the words of liturgical proclamation are more accurately understood when we view them as "performative," as accomplishing the work of salvation that they describe even as the reader proclaims them. The word of God is not a history lesson, though there is history in it. The word is not a story, though it is full of stories. It is not a set of rules to live by, though there is much in it to guide our choices. No, the word of God is a living and dynamic presence, achieving the very salvation about which it speaks even as the reader proclaims it. The church has taught us this view in the words "Christ is present in his word since it is he himself who speaks when the holy scriptures are read in the church." And again, "In the liturgy God speaks to his people and Christ is still proclaiming his gospel" (Vatican II, *The Constitution on the Liturgy*).

In the reader's proclamation, the word of God is alive with power, achieving the sanctification of the people to whom it is proclaimed and rendering glory to the very God whose creative word brought all things into being.

2 *Effective Communication Skills*

With the tremendous growth in our ability to share information around the world (through radio, television, videotape, telecommunications and computer networking), there is more emphasis today on "live" communication (as opposed to the silent, printed word) than perhaps ever before. And with that emphasis has come an ever deepening awareness of what makes communication effective — as well as what compromises its effectiveness. The minister of the word at liturgical celebrations is, in some sense, challenged in gaining the attention of a culture completely awash in a sea of voices and, to use a popular buzz phrase, "sound bytes."

The implication is obvious: While respecting the unique purpose of liturgical proclamation (communal celebration of faith), modern ministers of the word must develop a very high degree of skill in order to gain credibility with their audiences. People who hear professional speakers through various media every day — and who are in control of the off/on buttons and volume controls — are naturally more demanding in their expectations of any speaker or reader who presumes to command their attention. *All the communication skills relevant to public speaking are relevant to liturgical proclamation.* In no way does this emphatic statement imply that the purposes of public speaking and liturgical proclamation are identical; they are not. The purpose of liturgical proclamation (and all liturgy) is ritual celebration of faith. It is not to inform, to persuade or to entertain (though it may do all three). Nevertheless, the skills required for effective proclamation are the same as those we expect to witness in public speakers recognized for their ability to communicate effectively. These skills are studied at length here, and exercises for developing them are provided, always with particular attention to how they apply to the liturgy and to the proclamation of sacred scripture.

The phenomenon of language

Human language and speech is such a wondrous phenomenon that we need to remind ourselves from time to time of just how mysterious, complex and powerful it is. As human beings, we use it every day, and we take it for granted. But as ministers of the word, we should perhaps take a moment to marvel at the miracle of communication that separates our species from all others. We come face to face with its potential power every time we proclaim the scriptures.

Those who study language at its very core and origins can do little more than speculate about how and when it came to be and how it appears in such amazing diversity among the peoples of the earth. They remind us that all language is primarily spoken and heard, and only secondarily is it a written code. Ritual proclamation clearly asserts this fundamental understanding of human communication as an immediate exchange between the human voice and the human ear. It is "live" communication. Silent consultation of a printed text (the missals of earlier days, the missalettes of today) during liturgy compromises the immediacy of liturgical proclamation.

Theories about how language came to be are diverse. Some scholars believe that all speech and language are learned, while others theorize that the human organism comes equipped at birth with an innate language "program" that develops simultaneously with physical growth. In any case, it is clear that language and speech are far more than simple codes that enable human beings to trade information. Language and speech are phenomena through which we share and express our similarities and differences, our emotions, our very lives.

The most remarkable assertion about language is that it may well be coterminous with thought. It may well have been the development of language that enabled *homo sapiens* (our species) to evolve — and the lack of it that accounts for the disappearance of other species. The hypothesis, in question form, would read something like this: Which came first, thought or language? Did the development of language make sequential thought patterns possible, or did the rise of such patterns create a need for, and the development of, language? We may never be able to answer such questions completely. The point for our present consideration is that language and speech are incredibly complex, radically humanizing phenomena, and our ministry as readers can only be enhanced by our willingness to appreciate their power and subtlety, indeed, their beauty and diversity.

The power of human speech

Our personal experience provides sufficient evidence for the power of human speech. We know that it can heal, destroy or provoke to anger. We have used it to express love, hate, disgust, ecstasy, anger, joy — the full range of human emotions. We have heard others speak and have known that it can affect us quite profoundly, for good or for ill. We have heard strong arguments spoken by trustworthy speakers who have changed our way of thinking and our choices. We have seen others swayed to poor choices by charlatans who have misused the power of speech.

In our ministry as readers we need to heighten our awareness of our power. Our proclamation of the word is *never* without an effect. The poorest proclamation, the mediocre proclamation and the most compelling proclamation each affect their hearers. What is true of liturgical worship is true of proclamation, of which it is a part: Poor liturgy diminishes faith; good liturgy augments it. A time-proven Latin axiom sums it up best: *Lex orandi, lex credendi* — as we pray, so shall we believe; the manner of our worship determines the quality of our belief.

But it is the potential of our power for good that we want to emphasize here. And to do that, we need to consider another aspect of human speech as it applies to our ministry. That aspect is its *sacramentality*. The familiar definition of sacrament as "an outward sign of an inward reality" can help us appreciate why the church invests the proclamation of the word with such significance. "It is Christ himself who speaks." Christ's word is creative and causative. The water poured at baptism and the words that are spoken ("I baptize you in the name of . . .") are the outward signs of the sacrament of baptism. The inward reality is the incorporation of the newly baptized into the church, the Body of Christ. Similarly, when the reader proclaims the good news in the liturgical context, the word goes forth from the reader and is fulfilled in the hearing of the assembly. An action takes place. The "sign," the proclamation, is outward. The fulfillment of the word even as it is proclaimed is the "inward reality."

This is not to say that the proclamation of the word is itself a sacrament. It does, though, have a sacramental character and effect, like the liturgy of which it is a part. In the words of the apostle Paul, "As often as you eat this bread and drink the cup, you proclaim the Lord's death until he comes" (1 Corinthians 11:26). The eucharist is more than a memorial, more than simply remembering what Christ accomplished in his death and resurrection. It is a continuation of that accomplishment throughout all time. Proclaiming the word is more than a retelling or a rereading. It is a continuation of God's saving intervention in human history.

Human speech is powerful. When it is employed in the proclamation of the word of God, it is sacramental. Readers who thus see the power and responsibility with which they are entrusted will not take their charism lightly.

The vocal mechanism

Anyone who speaks publicly needs a basic understanding of how the vocal mechanism works, how speech is produced. The reason for this is that human speech is a controlled function. That is, the speaker can use the mechanism to adjust many aspects of speech. Some cannot be adjusted: the natural timbre of the voice (which makes it recognizably distinct from others), the highness or depth of the tone (outside a certain range) and certain other innate qualities.

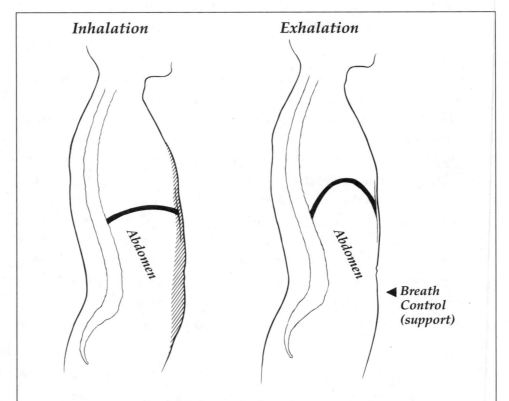

These simple drawings illustrate the importance of the abdominal muscles in supporting the column of air that produces speech. The diaphragm is a large flat muscle that separates the organs of the upper body from those of the abdomen. We do not control the diaphragm. It automatically contracts (flattens out) to produce an intake of breath by creating a vacuum in the chest (inhalation). Air rushes in to fill it. The diaphragm then relaxes so that air can escape (exhalation). The outflow of air produces sound when we speak. We control the outflow of air by gently drawing in our abdominal muscles, thus supporting the relaxed diaphragm and the column of air above it.

First among the adjustments that can be controlled is the relationship between phonation (making sounds in speech) and the inhalation/exhalation cycle — in other words, breath control. Accomplished singers know how important breath control is, and so do accomplished speakers. Liturgical readers must develop breath control in order to perform their ministry well.

Supporting the column of air (which creates sounds by passing through the vocal chords in the larynx) is a matter of contracting the abdominal wall (pulling the abdominal muscles) to support the relaxed diaphragm. Very often, beginning speakers need to be reminded that this is the only part of the body that should not be relaxed during speech. Nervousness and bad habits can create tension in the shoulders, neck and throat, which then constricts the breathing process and makes breath control and speech difficult. Learning to support speech with the abdominal wall is not difficult; learning to relax the rest of the body can be challenging.

Exercise

Here is a simple exercise that will increase breath control by increasing lung capacity and strengthening the abdominal wall. Stand comfortably erect, with good but relaxed posture. Breathe in slowly through your mouth on the count of four (one Mississippi, two Mississippi, three Mississippi, four Mississippi). The idea is to draw a full deep breath. The intake of breath should be completely silent; if you can hear it, you are breathing in too quickly. Be careful not to raise your shoulders or to exert any effort trying to expand your chest. And let the abdominal muscles relax completely. The incoming volume of air is all that accounts for movement. You should see some outward movement of both chest and belly.

Now you are going to exhale slowly on the count of eight (one Mississippi, etc.). Exhale through the teeth, making a hissing sound (sssssssssss). The sound should be very soft on the count of one and as loud as possible on the count of eight as you try to empty your lungs completely. During exhalation, conserve your air as you consciously but gently pull the abdomen in to support a steady outflow. The contraction of these muscles will increase as your volume increases. Once again, be very careful not to involve the chest, shoulder, head, neck or throat muscles. Do not collapse the shoulders, for example, as you run out of air. Isolate the abdominal muscles to do that work.

The exercise adds four counts to each subsequent exhalation:

Breathe in quietly through the mouth: four counts

Breathe out hissing, soft to loud: eight counts

Breathe in quietly through the nose: four counts

Breathe out hissing, soft to loud: twelve counts

Breathe in quietly through the nose: four counts

Breathe out hissing, soft to loud: sixteen counts

Breathe in quietly through the nose: four counts

Breathe out hissing, soft to loud: twenty counts

Breathe in quietly through the nose: four counts

Breathe out hissing, soft to loud: twenty-four counts

Breathe in quietly through the nose: four counts

Breathe out hissing, soft to loud: twenty-eight counts

And so on.

Caution! You may find yourself getting lightheaded rather quickly. Don't hyperventilate. Your ability to tolerate higher counts will increase with practice. Some will find that hissing on an exhalation for twenty-eight counts seems impossible. It's not. Professionals can go as high as forty counts. But remember that the exercise is a breath control builder, not an endurance contest!

Because the language of sacred scripture is exalted language, it often includes very lengthy sentences that can challenge the reader's breath control. Such sentences need to flow, dipping and bobbing through various levels of modifying clauses. To chop them up into smaller bits invariably robs them of their power. Here are a few sentences that will challenge and develop effective breath control. Remember to use your full proclamation voice when reading them and to employ the fullest range of vocal variety (melody). Otherwise, the point of the exercise will be lost. Finally, do not continue reading after all but a fraction of your breath is gone and your voice begins to sound shaky or pinched. The point is to sustain the natural, full sound as long as you can. You will soon notice that your reservoir is growing!

Exodus 19:16

On the morning of the third day
there was thunder and lightning,
as well as a thick cloud on the mountain,
and a blast of a trumpet so loud
that all the people who were in the camp trembled.

Genesis 11:6

And the LORD said, "Look, they are one people,
and they have all one language;
and this is only the beginning of what they will do;
nothing that they propose to do
    will now be impossible for them.

For the following passages, note that you are not expected to proclaim them in just one breath. But it's a good exercise. Passages like these often suffer from a choppy delivery. See how fluid you can make them by using good breath control.

Proverbs 8:27 – 31

When he established the heavens, I was there,
when he drew a circle on the face of the deep,
when he made firm the skies above,
when he established the fountains of the deep,
when he assigned to the sea its limit,
so that the waters might not transgress his command,
when he marked out the foundations of the earth,
then I was beside him, like a master worker;
and I was daily his delight,
rejoicing before him always,
rejoicing in his inhabited world
and delighting in the human race.

1 Corinthians 1:22 – 24

For Jews demand signs and Greeks desire wisdom,
but we proclaim Christ crucified,
a stumbling block to Jews and foolishness to Gentiles,
but to those who are the called, both Jews and Greeks,
Christ the power of God and the wisdom of God.

Revelation 1:9 – 11a

I, John, your brother
who share with you in Jesus
the persecution and the kingdom and the patient endurance,
was on the island called Patmos
because of the word of God and the testimony of Jesus.
I was in the spirit on the Lord's day,
and I heard behind me a loud voice like a trumpet
saying, "Write in a book what you see
and send it to the seven churches."

Isaiah 58:6 – 10

Thus says the Lord:
"Is this not the fast that I choose:
to loose the bonds of injustice,
to undo the thongs of the yoke,
to let the oppressed go free,
and to break every yoke?
Is it not to share your bread with the hungry,
and bring the homeless poor into your house;
when you see the naked, to cover them,
and not to hide yourself from your own kin?

"Then your light shall break forth like the dawn,
and your healing shall spring up quickly;
your vindicator shall go before you,
the glory of the Lord shall be your rear guard.
Then you shall call, and the Lord will answer;
you shall cry for help, and he will say, 'Here I am.'

"If you remove the yoke from among you,
the pointing of the finger, the speaking of evil,
if you offer your food to the hungry
and satisfy the needs of the afflicted,
then your light shall rise in the darkness
and your gloom be like the noonday."

Deuteronomy 5:12 – 15

The Lord says this:
"Observe the sabbath day and keep it holy,

as the Lord your God commanded you.
Six days you shall labor and do all your work.

"But the seventh day is a sabbath to the Lord your God;
you shall not do any work—
you, or your son or your daughter,
   or your male or female slave,
or your ox or your donkey, or any of your livestock,
or the resident alien in your towns,
so that your male and female slave may rest as well as you.

"Remember that you were a slave in the land of Egypt,
and the Lord your God brought you out from there
with a mighty hand and an outstretched arm;
therefore the Lord your God commanded you to keep the
   sabbath day."

Vocal variety

Communication specialists tell us that the single most important quality demanded by an audience is vocal variety. What audiences find most difficult to listen to is a monotone voice that lacks color, variations in pitch, animation or warmth.

Vocal variety is an umbrella term that includes all the characteristics of speech that will be discussed here. It includes melody (or modulation), rate, pause, volume, articulation—and this list is not exhaustive. Each term is elusive and imprecise. What is "too fast"? How loud is "too loud"? When does a pause become "dead space"? In our discussion of vocal variety, keep in mind that the complexities of human speech sounds do not categorize precisely. Matters of taste, individual preferences and many other considerations make the aesthetics of speech a very imprecise science! Nevertheless, we can speak of what is effective, pleasant and generally considered "listenable." We also can identify undesirable characteristics: being monotonous, inaudible, unclear, artificial, phony or stereotypical.

As you study the individual components of vocal variety, keep in mind that they are interdependent. After all, they cannot be considered or experienced in isolation. The melody of the passage will influence the rate at which it is proclaimed, and effective pausing depends on how fast or slow the text is read—as does good articulation. Although the volume at which you read must always be adequate and appropriate, it cannot always be the same. Melody, rate and articulation all affect considerations of loudness and softness.

The following passages require a lot of vocal modulation to communicate the various levels of syntax or the appropriate range of feelings. Don't be afraid to exaggerate vocal range in these exercises, realizing, of course, that in actual proclamation such exaggeration would be out of the question.

Notice that this first passage contains a rhetorical question and that contrasts are involved ("not with water *only* but with water and the *blood*").

1 John 5:5 – 6

Who is it that conquers the world
but the one who believes that Jesus is the Son of God?
This is the one who came by water and blood, Jesus Christ,
not with the water only but with the water and the blood.
And the Spirit is the one that testifies,
for the Spirit is the truth.

In the next passage, note that the word *faith* is italicized to indicate that it is the recurring theme; a well-modulated and varied delivery will make the word fresh each time, not as though it were a new idea each time but the same idea with another aspect. By the time you say the word the last couple of times, it should feel and sound like "an old friend."

Hebrews 11:1 – 9

Now *faith* is the assurance of things hoped for,
the conviction of things not seen.
Indeed, by *faith* our ancestors received approval.

By *faith* we understand
that the worlds were prepared by the word of God,
so that what is seen was made from things that are not visible.

By *faith* Abel offered to God
a more acceptable sacrifice than Cain's.
Through this he received approval as righteous,
God himself giving approval to his gifts;
he died, but through his *faith* he still speaks.

By *faith* Enoch was taken so that he did not experience death;
and "he was not found, because God had taken him."

For it was attested before he was taken away
that "he had pleased God."

And without *faith* it is impossible to please God,
for whoever would approach him must believe
that he exists and that he rewards those who seek him.

By *faith* Noah, warned by God about events as yet unseen,
respected the warning and built an ark to save his household;
by this he condemned the world
and became an heir to the righteousness
that is in accordance with *faith*.

By *faith* Abraham obeyed
when he was called to set out for a place
that he was to receive as an inheritance;
and he set out, not knowing where he was going.

By *faith* he stayed for a time
in the land he had been promised,
as in a foreign land, living in tents,
as did Isaac and Jacob,
who were heirs with him of the same promise.

Melody

Melody is a word associated with music, of course, and thus it is perhaps
the best term to use in discussing this aspect of vocal variation. It is also
a risky word, though, because when it is applied to speech it can tend to
make us think of "sing-song." But melody in music refers to the movement of the pitch from one level to another — the kind of movement
that must also typify the voice of the reader. When melody and lyric
complement one another, as they do in the work of any good composer,
each serves to augment and enhance the other. Nothing less is required
in reading aloud.

Here is a particularly beautiful text from Paul's First Letter to the
Corinthians. It is a hymn to love. The challenge for the reader is to treat
it like the quasi-musical text that it is without sounding ridiculous or
affected. Experiment broadly in your reading of this text. Consider even
making up a simple tune to sing it by. Discover new ways to make each
characteristic of love (patient, kind, not envious) stand on its own. The
text demands a lot of "vocal music," but that music must not obscure
the meaning.

1 Corinthians 13:3 – 13

If I give away all my possessions,
and if I hand over my body so that I may boast,
but do not have love, I gain nothing.

Love is patient; love is kind;
love is not envious or boastful or arrogant or rude.
It does not insist on its own way;
it is not irritable or resentful;
it does not rejoice in wrongdoing,
but rejoices in the truth.
It bears all things, believes all things,
hopes all things, endures all things.
Love never ends.

But as for prophecies, they will come to an end;
as for tongues, they will cease;
as for knowledge, it will come to an end.

For we know only in part, and we prophesy only in part;
but when the complete comes, the partial will come
    to an end.
When I was a child, I spoke like a child,
I thought like a child, I reasoned like a child;
when I became an adult, I put an end to childish ways.
For now we see in a mirror, dimly,
but then we will see face to face.
Now I know only in part;
then I will know fully, even as I have been fully known.

Now faith, hope, and love abide, these three;
and the greatest of these is love.

For contrast, read the following passage aloud, noting the difference between it and the previous passage in terms of the degree and kind of melody required.

Acts 2:42 – 47

They devoted themselves to the apostles' teaching
    and fellowship,
to the breaking of bread and the prayers.

Awe came upon everyone,
because many wonders and signs were being done
    by the apostles.

All who believed were together and had all things
    in common;
they would sell their possessions and goods
and distribute the proceeds to all, as any had need.
Day by day, as they spent much time together in the temple,
they broke bread at home
and ate their food with glad and generous hearts,
praising God and having the goodwill of all the people.
And day by day the Lord added to their number
those who were being saved.

Jeremiah 33:14 – 16

The days are surely coming, says the Lord,
when I will fulfill the promise
I made to the house of Israel
and the house of Judah.

In those days and at that time
I will cause a righteous Branch to spring up for David;
and he shall execute justice and righteousness in the land.

In those days Judah will be saved
and Jerusalem will live in safety.
And this is the name by which it will be called:
"The Lord is our righteousness."

2 Corinthians 3:1 – 6

We do not need, as some do,
letters of recommendation to you or from you, do we?
You yourselves are our letter, written on our hearts,
to be known and read by all;
and you show that you are a letter of Christ, prepared by us,
written not with ink but with the Spirit of the living God,
not on tablets of stone but on tablets of human hearts.

Such is the confidence that we have through Christ
    toward God.
Not that we are competent of ourselves
to claim anything as coming from us;

our competence is from God,
who has made us competent to be ministers
    of a new covenant,
not of letter but of spirit;
for the letter kills, but the Spirit gives life.

Malachi 4:1 – 2

The Lord says this:
"See, the day is coming, burning like an oven,
when all the arrogant and all evildoers will be stubble;
the day that comes shall burn them up,"
    says the Lord of hosts,
"So that it will leave them neither root nor branch.

"But for you who revere my name
the sun of righteousness shall rise,
with healing in its wings."

Clearly, some texts require a great deal more melody than others. However, there is melody in every text. The difference is determined largely by the difference in the kind of prose we're dealing with. Paul's "hymn to love" is clearly poetic. The passage from Acts is clearly narrative. Melody is determined by such factors as topic, mood, purpose and literary genre (poetry, prose, narrative, argument). Generally, the more exalted the subject matter, the broader the melody patterns. But excesses are easy to spot, and some restraint and objectivity must always characterize ritual proclamation. Your purpose is to proclaim the text, not to re-create or dramatize it. Above all, it is the sense and *feeling* of the passage that must guide you in all matters pertaining to effective communication.

Rate

Everyone reads too fast. Well, perhaps not everyone, but this is surely the most common complaint registered against readers. Audience sensitivity is the answer. You have the printed words before you (words you presumably have studied closely) and the assembly does not. They are relying on aural stimulation alone. (If they do have the text before them in a missalette, your challenge is to make "hearing" more profitable and enjoyable than "reading along.")

The concept of "rate" involves more than looking at whether something is fast or slow. Like "melody," the term "rate" also can be associated with music and rhythm. So when we speak of how quickly or how slowly the reader reads, we are considering more than just how long it takes the reader to get from the first word of the passage to the last. Music teaches us rather quickly (almost intuitively) that rhythm is interesting when it is varied and not particularly interesting when it lapses into a steady beat without variation. There are instances, of course, when an almost hypnotic rhythm serves music; the same is true of some scripture passages. Perhaps the most obvious example is the genealogy of Jesus as recorded by Matthew, an important section of the gospel tradition but one which, because of its length and its challenging pronunciations, is often skipped.

Matthew 1:1 – 17

An account of the genealogy of Jesus the Messiah,
the son of David, the son of Abraham.

Abraham was the father of Isaac,
Isaac the father of Jacob,
Jacob the father of Judah and his brothers,
Judah the father of Perez and Zerah by Tamar,
Perez the father of Hezron,
Hezron the father of Aram,
Aram the father of Aminadab,
Aminadab the father of Nahshon,
Nahshon the father of Salmon,
Salmon the father of Boaz by Rahab,
Boaz the father of Obed by Ruth,
Obed the father of Jesse,
and Jesse the father of Kind David.

And David was the father of Solomon by the wife of Uriah,
Solomon the father of Rehoboam,
Rehoboam the father of Abijah,
Abijah the father of Asaph,
Asaph the father of Jehoshaphat,
Jehoshaphat the father of Joram,
Joram the father of Uzziah,
Uzziah the father of Jotham,
Jotham the father of Ahaz,
Ahaz the father of Hezekiah,
Hezekiah the father of Manasseh,
Manasseh the father of Amos,
Amos father of Josiah,

and Josiah the father of Jechoniah and his brothers,
at the time of the deportation to Babylon.

After the deportation to Babylon,
Jechoniah was the father of Salathiel,
Salathiel the father of Zerubbabel,
Zerubbabel the father of Abiud,
Abiud the father of Eliakim,
Eliakim the father of Azor,
Azor the father of Zadok,
Zadok the father of Achim,
Achim the father of Eliud,
Eliud the father of Eleazar,
Eleazar the father of Matthan,
Matthan the father of Jacob,
and Jacob the father of Joseph the husband of Mary,
of whom Jesus was born,
who is called the Messiah.

So all the generations
from Abraham to David are fourteen generations;
from David to the deportation to Babylon,
    fourteen generations;
from the deportation to Babylon to the Messiah,
fourteen generations.

Pronunciation guide for the genealogy:

Perez: PEE-rehz
Zerah: ZEE-reh
Tamar: TAY-mer
Hezron: HEHZ-ruhn
Ram: ram
Amminadab: ah-MIHN-uh-dab
Nahshon: NAH-shuhn
Salmon: SAL-muhn
Boaz: BO-az
Rahab: RAY-hab
Obed: O-bed
Abijah: uh-BAI-dzhuh
Asa: AY-suh
Jehoshaphat: dzhee-HAHSH-uh-fat
Joram: DZHO-ram
Uzziah: yoo-ZEI-uh
Jotham: DZHO-thuhm

Ahaz: AY-haz
Hezekiah: heh-zeh-KAI-uh
Manasseh: man-AS-eh
Amos: AY-muhs
Josiah: dzho-SAI-uh
Jechoniah: dzhehk-o-NAI-uh
Shealtiel: shee-AL-tih-ehl
Zerubbabel: zeh-RUH-buh-behl
Abiud: uh-BAI-uhd
Eliakim: ee-LAI-uh-kihm
Azor: AY-zawr
Zadok: ZAY-dahk
Achim: AY-kihm
Eliud: ee-LAI-uhd
Eleazar: ehl-ee-AY-zer
Matthan: MAT-than

Clearly, the evangelist's intention is to create a steady beat, as
though to enable us to experience the inexorable march of generations

down through the ages leading to the birth of Jesus. It would be a mistake not to respect this intention, though some instruction to the hearers beforehand may be necessary to enable them to appreciate the structure and purpose of this unusual text.

We are not often faced with such extraordinary texts. But consider another literary device employed throughout many books of the Hebrew scriptures: parallelism. It is a way of writing in which each statement is echoed, paralleled or expanded upon in the next. Here is a classic example in which the text has been arranged to illustrate the parallelism:

Joel 2:1 – 10

Blow the trumpet in Zion;
   sound the alarm on my holy mountain!
Let all the inhabitants of the land tremble,
   for the day of the LORD is coming, it is near —
   a day of darkness and gloom,
   a day of clouds and thick darkness!

Like blackness spread upon the mountains
   a great and powerful army comes;
their like has never been from of old,
   nor will be again after them in ages to come.

Fire devours in front of them,
   and behind them a flame burns.
Before them the land is like the garden of Eden,
   but after them a desolate wilderness,
    and nothing escapes them.

They have the appearance of horses,
   and like war-horses they charge.
As with the rumbling of chariots,
   they leap on the tops of the mountains,
like the crackling of a flame of fire devouring the stubble,
   like a powerful army drawn up for battle.

Before them peoples are in anguish,
   all faces grow pale.
Like warriors they charge,
   like soldiers they scale the wall.
Each keeps to its own course,
   they do not swerve from their paths.
They do not jostle one another,

each keeps to its own track;
they burst through the weapons
　　and are not halted.
They leap upon the city,
　　they run upon the walls;
they climb up into the houses,
　　they enter through the windows like a thief.
The earth quakes before them,
　　the heavens tremble.
The sun and the moon are darkened,
　　and the stars withdraw their shining.

It is not difficult to see and hear the chant-like rhythm intended by the author. Read the text aloud while keeping in mind that each indented line echoes or expands upon the one before it; the lines share a parallel thought or image. The rate at which any such passage should be proclaimed is largely determined by its structure. Each pair of lines is separated from the others in a way different from the lesser separation within the pair. Although the rhythm may be constant, or at least patterned, the reading will be varied by other vocal elements: melody, pauses, and so forth, all dictated by the varied meanings and feelings of each set of parallel texts.

And what about those very brief readings that almost seem over before they begin? Rate is an important consideration in such cases.

Practicing rate

Some texts require a slower proclamation simply because they are dense in meaning or in syntax. Others are particularly solemn or particularly brief. A very brief reading must be proclaimed slowly, lest it be over before the hearers have had a chance to focus on it. Still other readings can profit from a degree of briskness. Consider the following passage, the second reading on the Feast of the Holy Trinity (Year A). It is one of the briefest readings in the entire lectionary. It should take between 40 and 45 seconds to proclaim effectively, including the opening announcement and concluding dialogue. Time yourself.

2 Corinthians 13:11 – 13

A reading from the Second Letter of Paul to the Corinthians.

Brothers and sisters,
put things in order, listen to my appeal,

agree with one another,
live in peace;
and the God of love and peace will be with you.
Greet one another with a holy kiss.
All the saints greet you.

The grace of the Lord Jesus Christ,
the love of God,
and the communion of the Holy Spirit
be with all of you.

The word of the Lord.

Pausing

The challenge in effective pausing is learning not to fear silence. Many readers, especially those who are new to the ministry, are afraid of the "sound of silence" when they are at the lectern. A steady stream of sound gives them the impression that they are moving along nicely and not stumbling over starts and stops. Unfortunately, the "steady stream of sound" is not pleasant for the hearers and does violence to the text. Remember that your audience must process the text, relying on your vocal presentation to endow it with meaning, to signal changes in topic, to prepare them for a particularly significant part of the reading, and so forth. Effective pausing gives them time to do their processing. It also gives you time to refresh your understanding and your voice. Finally, a well-executed pause is one way to emphasize part of a text — either what has just been proclaimed or what is to come next; this is the "pause for effect."

Lively human speech, of whatever degree of formality, is punctuated with pauses, very much like the "rests" in music. Some are very brief, almost imperceptible; others are quite long and dramatic. We even speak of the "pregnant pause" to describe a moment of hesitation that is filled with meaning. The point is that we are speaking of nothing exotic here, nothing peculiar to public speaking or to proclamation. Like music, natural human speech derives a great part of its meaning from the silences that punctuate the sound.

Consider the following reading from the Acts of the Apostles on the Fifth Sunday of Easter (Year B). Here is an instance where we might employ three kinds of pauses, each signaling something different.

Acts 9:26–31

When Saul had come to Jerusalem,
he attempted to join the disciples;

[slight pause for effect]

and they were all *afraid* of him,
for they did not *believe* that he was a *disciple*.
But Barnabas took him,
brought him to the apostles,
and described for them how on the road
    he had seen the Lord,
who had spoken to him,
and how in Damascus he had spoken boldly
    in the name of Jesus.

So Saul went in and out among them in Jerusalem,
speaking boldly in the name of the Lord.

[longer pause: new but related topic]

He spoke and argued with the Hellenists;
but they were attempting to kill him.
When the believers learned of it,
they brought Saul down to Caesarea
    and sent him off to Tarsus.

[significant pause: completely new topic]

Meanwhile the church throughout Judea, Galilee, and Samaria
had peace and was built up.
Living in the fear of the Lord
and in the comfort of the Holy Spirit,
it increased in numbers.

How long really is a "brief" pause, a "significant" pause, and so on? The subtlety of the spoken word makes it inadvisable (even impossible) to apply anything like a mathematical value to vocal elements (count to one, count to three) or even to use arbitrary markings (/ = brief pause; // = medium pause; /// = long pause). Any such system is subject to individual or idiosyncratic interpretation. A demonstration by a seasoned and well-received reader can help, but that is not always available. The best guarantee that you will employ pauses and all the elements of vocal variety is threefold: (1) your sensitivity to spoken language and how it works; (2) your thorough understanding of the text; and (3) your courageous desire to share it fully with your audience.

In Isaiah's poignant exhortation to accept God's benevolence and love, the text is almost disjointed. In its fervor it rephrases itself, introduces new images, asks rhetorical questions, and so forth. Without careful pausing, the text could sound like a jumble of thoughts and be difficult to follow. But a careful delivery will reveal an earnest and heartfelt plea that becomes stronger as it proceeds. Markings suggest one possible approach.

Isaiah 55:1–3

Everyone who thirsts, come to the waters; // and you that have no money, come, / buy and eat! /// Come, / buy wine and milk without money and without price. ///

Why do you spend your money for that which is not bread, / and your labor for that which does not satisfy? // Listen carefully to me, and eat what is good, /and delight yourselves in rich food. ///

Incline your ear, and come to me; / listen, so that you may live. // I will make with you an everlasting covenant, // my steadfast, sure love for David.

Further exercises for practicing pausing

Philippians 1:3–6, 8–11

My brothers and sisters,
I thank my God every time I remember you,
constantly praying with joy
in every one of my prayers for all of you,
because of your sharing in the gospel
from the first day until now.

I am confident of this,
that the one who began a good work among you
will bring it to completion by the day of Jesus Christ.

For God is my witness,
how I long for all of you
with the compassion of Christ Jesus.
And this is my prayer,
that your love may overflow more and more
with knowledge and full insight

so that in the day of Christ
you may be pure and blameless,
having produced the harvest of righteousness
that comes through Jesus Christ
for the glory and praise of God.

Matthew 5:1 – 12a

When Jesus saw the crowds, he went up the mountain;
and after he sat down, his disciples came to him.
Then he began to speak, and he taught them, saying:
"Blessed are the poor in spirit,
for theirs is the kingdom of heaven.
Blessed are those who mourn,
for they will be comforted.
Blessed are the meek,
for they will inherit the earth.
Blessed are those who hunger and thirst for righteousness,
for they will be filled.

"Blessed are the merciful,
for they will receive mercy.
Blessed are the pure in heart,
for they will see God.
Blessed are the peacemakers,
for they will be called children of God.
Blessed are those who are persecuted
    for righteousness' sake,
for theirs is the kingdom of heaven.

"Blessed are you when people revile you and persecute you
and utter all kinds of evil against you falsely on my account.
Rejoice and be glad,
for your reward is great in heaven,
for in the same way they persecuted the prophets
who were before you."

Exodus 20:1 – 3, 7 – 8, 12 – 17

God spoke all these words:
I am the Lord your God,
who brought you out of the land of Egypt,
out of the house of slavery;
you shall have no other gods before me.

You shall not make wrongful use of the name of the Lord
   your God,
for the Lord will not acquit anyone who misuses his name.

Remember the sabbath day, and keep it holy.

Honor your father and your mother,
so that your days may be long in the land
that the Lord your God is giving you.

You shall not murder.
You shall not commit adultery.
You shall not steal.
You shall not bear false witness against your neighbor.
You shall not covet your neighbor's house;
you shall not covet your neighbor's wife,
or male or female slave, or ox, or donkey,
or anything that belongs to your neighbor.

Volume (pitch and projection)

The principle of audience sensitivity permeates all our considerations. All communication, at every instant, should be understood and represented as a circle.

Speaker   Audience

Both speaker and audience are constantly sending signals; the circular flow of information and feedback is constant. The difference between the two is that the communicator is ordinarily sending verbal signals, whereas the audience is sending nonverbal signals. The effective communicator must remain constantly alert to this feedback. We all hear liturgical readers who cannot be heard and who are apparently unaware that they cannot be heard. They seem, in fact, to be unaware that they have an audience. Such readers approach their task as one-sided. They send out signals but do not receive signals. The communication act is incomplete.

   As a reader you must remain aware of how your hearers are responding. Are they attentive? Are they distracted by something else?

Are they nodding off? Are they finding seats because they came in late? Are they paging through missalettes to find the printed text of what they can't hear?

The reason contemporary audiences will not tolerate insufficient volume is that they ordinarily do not have to. In informal conversation they can ask their communication partner to speak up. Radios, televisions and other sound media have volume controls. If your reading is simply not loud enough, then something else is being perceived as louder. And that something else could be crying infants, the air-conditioning system, a restless congregation or the "inner noise" that we all have playing in our heads at every moment. The point is, if something is louder (let alone more interesting or more commanding of attention), the reading will not be heard.

But sheer volume is not the answer. Indeed, excessive volume is more disagreeable than insufficient volume. The kind of volume required in public communication situations is more complex than the turn of a knob, either on the microphone system or in the human body! Just as important as sound level is sound "height" and "weight," or pitch and projection. Depending on the environment in which your ministry is exercised (cathedral or chapel), the "height," or pitch, of the voice must be elevated accordingly. And the voice must take on a proportionate degree of "weight," or projection strength, as well.

Let's say you are sitting on your back porch with your neighbor, engaged in conversation, watching your young children play on the swing set in the back yard. How would your voice sound as you and your neighbor swapped stories? Now you notice that Robby is pushing Mark's swing too high, so you call out, "Not so high, Rob!" How does your voice sound now? Not only is it louder, it's higher (pitch) and weightier (projection). This situation is not so different from any public communication situation to which your voice must adapt. Sheer volume (loudness) is not sufficient. Otherwise, the volume control on the public address system could solve the problem. Imagine how your quiet conversation with your neighbor would sound booming through a microphone system. A trifle ridiculous, to say the least. And yet, many readers and speakers seem to think they can speak in a normal conversational tone at the lectern because the microphone does all the work. For liturgical readers, it helps to recall that our ministry is called "proclamation."

The following texts are good for practicing sufficient projection. They were obviously proclaimed (even declaimed) in their original settings. There should be no sense that you are re-enacting the original situation, of course, but the tone of your voice should echo the "weight" of the occasion and the text itself. The exultation in Zephaniah's voice calls from the reader something more than a storyteller's tone. Imagine how inappropriate (almost laughable) these words would sound if they were muttered quietly or without expression. But notice also that the mood changes in the second paragraph. A sensitive reader would not read both paragraphs the same way. Experiment broadly with this text and don't be afraid of exaggerating it as you practice. Nothing even approaching exaggeration should appear in your proclamation of it, of course, but the voice and the body "remember" the energy of an exaggerated rehearsal and retain it.

Zephaniah 3:14 – 18a

Sing aloud, O daughter Zion; shout, O Israel!
Rejoice and exult with all your heart,
O daughter Jerusalem!
The LORD has taken away the judgments against you,
he has turned away your enemies.
The king of Israel, the LORD, is in your midst;
you shall fear disaster no more.

On that day it shall be said to Jerusalem:
Do not fear, O Zion;
do not let your hands grow weak.
The LORD, your God, is in your midst,
a warrior who gives victory;
he will rejoice over you with gladness,
he will renew you in his love;
The LORD, your God, will exult over you with loud singing
as on a day of festival.

Exercise for practicing volume

Consider, for contrast, this gentle text from Isaiah. A favorite of many, it progresses from a quiet (but still heard!) opening to an exultant passage, then to an exhortation and concludes with a strong assertion of confidence. Question: How do you begin this reading gently and yet ensure that it will be heard by all? Answer: Pause for a significant amount of time after announcing the reading, looking at the assembly. Silence sometimes commands attention very effectively.

Isaiah 40:1–11

Comfort, O comfort my people,
says your God.
Speak tenderly to Jerusalem,
and cry to her
that she has served her term,
that her penalty is paid,
that she has received from the Lord's hand
double for all her sins.

[Obvious elevation of volume here:]

A voice cries out:
"In the wilderness prepare the way of the LORD,
make straight in the desert a highway for our God.
Every valley shall be lifted up,
and every mountain and hill be made low;
the uneven ground shall become level,
and the rough places a plain.
Then the glory of the LORD shall be revealed,
and all people shall see it together,
for the mouth of the LORD has spoken."

[And perhaps another here:]

A voice says, "Cry out!"
And I said, "What shall I cry?"
All people are grass,
their constancy is like the flower of the field.

[Sudden slight decrease in volume here?]

The grass withers, the flower fades,
when the breath of the LORD blows upon it;
surely the people are grass.
The grass withers, the flower fades;
but the word of our God will stand forever.

[Clearly, something new is required here:]

Get you up to a high mountain,
O Zion, herald of good tidings;
lift up your voice with strength,
O Jerusalem, herald of good tidings,
lift it up, do not fear;
say to the cities of Judah,
"Here is your God!"

[Quiet strength? Bold affirmation?]

See, the Lord GOD comes with might,
and his arm rules for him;
his reward is with him,
and his recompense before him.
He will feed his flock like a shepherd;
he will gather the lambs in his arms,
and carry them in his bosom,
and gently lead the mother sheep.

The appropriate volume for this passage will not be the same throughout. But be careful: Even the most tender words must be heard clearly by the worshiper farthest from you; yet the exhortation should not blast those nearby. Variances in volume in liturgical proclamation are subtle but nonetheless effective. Remember also that all the elements of vocal variety work together. A rise in volume is usually accompanied by a rise in pitch, a higher energy level, more forceful projection, a slightly slower or faster pace, and so forth.

Articulation

Articulation involves the "shape," or formation, of sounds with the lips, tongue, teeth, soft palate and muscles of the face. The way sounds are formed results in either clarity or mushiness, affectation or naturalness. What we recognize as a foreign or regional accent is the result of sounds being shaped in a way different from our own. There is no absolute rule of "right" and "wrong" in such matters. In some parts of the country, the reader who pronounces "walking" as "walkin'," and "others" as "othuhs," would be judged to have poor (or regional) articulation. "Where is she from?" the hearers would wonder. In other places, "walkin'" and "othuhs" would be expected and pass unnoticed. "Walking" and "others" would sound affected. More important than notions of correctness, from the audience's point of view, are clarity and the fulfillment of expectations.

Far more distracting than any unfamiliar accent or even error is exaggerated or overdone articulation. This is always perceived as phony or artificial, and it signals that the reader is more concerned with "getting it right" than with "getting it across."

With all of the above in mind, it may indeed be necessary for some readers to improve their articulation. Lazy articulation can muffle sounds and make words difficult to understand. Further evidence that all the elements of vocal variety are interdependent is that articulation almost always improves when the energy level is elevated through sufficient volume, pitch and projection.

Read the following passage aloud, paying particular attention to how you are forming the words. Do this several times. Demonstrate to yourself what you would consider "lazy" articulation, "pedantic" articulation and "regional" articulation. Try Texan, unless you're in Texas; otherwise try Brooklyn! The purpose of this exercise is to heighten your sensitivity to articulation. The goal of improved articulation is to sound natural and clear to your audience.

Luke 11:1 – 4

Jesus was praying in a certain place,
and after he had finished, one of his disciples said to him,
"Lord, teach us to pray,
as John taught his disciples."

He said to them, "When you pray, say:
'Father, hallowed be your name.
Your kingdom come.
Give us each day our daily bread.
And forgive us our sins,
for we ourselves forgive everyone indebted to us.
And do not bring us to the time of trial.'"

Do not confuse articulation with pronunciation. Pronunciation is a matter of what we have more or less agreed upon as the correct way to sound out a given word. "Irrelevant" is mispronounced if you say "irrevelant," regardless of how you articulate it. "Undoubtebly" is a common mispronunciation of "undoubtedly." Acceptable pronunciations are found in the dictionary; acceptable articulations are found in your mouth — and are exemplified in the speech of people in your part of the country who are widely regarded as effective speakers.

Another associated term is "enunciation." Its meaning is very similar to "articulation" but, unfortunately, conjures up in many minds the kind of exaggeration and artificiality that draws attention to itself and away from the text being read.

Exercise for articulation

The following passage is the first reading on the Feast of Pentecost. Although some readers dread it because of the proper names, it provides a good exercise in confident and clear articulation for other reasons, too. It contains energetic words that require energetic articulation: *rush, filled, bewildered, amazed, astonished, power* and so forth. The proper names must roll off the tongue with total confidence; otherwise, the hearers will be distracted as they root for you to get through the list! Master the names; then imbue the text with the kind of conviction that confident articulation makes possible.

Acts 2:1 – 11

When the day of Pentecost had come,
they were all together in one place.
And suddenly from heaven there came a sound
like the rush of a violent wind,
and it filled the entire house where they were sitting.
Divided tongues, as of fire, appeared among them,
and a tongue rested on each of them.
All of them were filled with the Holy Spirit
and began to speak in other languages,
as the Spirit gave them ability.

Now there were devout Jews from every nation under heaven
living in Jerusalem.
And at this sound the crowd gathered and was bewildered,
because all heard them speaking in their own languages.
Amazed and astonished, they asked,
"Are not all these who are speaking Galileans?
And how is it that we hear, each of us,
in our own language?
Parthians, Medes, Elamites,
and residents of Mesopotamia,
Judea and Cappadocia, Pontus and Asia,
Phrygia and Pamphylia,
Egypt and the parts of Libya belonging to Cyrene,
and visitors from Rome, both Jews and converts,
Cretans and Arabs —
     in our own languages we hear them
     speaking about God's deeds of power."

Pronunciation guide:

Galileans = gal-ih-LEE-uhnz
Parthians = PAHR-thee-uhnz
Medes = meeds
Elamites = EE-luh-maits

Mesopotamia = mehs-o-po-TAY-mihuh
Judea = dzhoo-DEE-uh
Cappadocia = kap-ih-DO-shee-uh
Pontus = PAHN-tuhs

Phrygia = FRIH-dzhih-uh   Cyrene = sai-REE-nee
Pamphylia = pam-FIHL-ih-uh Cretans = KREE-tihnz
Libya = LIH-bih-uh   Arabs = EHR-uhbz (not AY-rabz!)

Hebrews 7:23 – 28

The priests of the first covenant were many in number,
because they were prevented by death from continuing
    in office;
but Jesus holds his priesthood permanently,
because he continues forever.
Consequently he is able for all time
to save those who approach God through him,
since he always lives to make intercession for them.

For it was fitting that we should have such a high priest,
holy, blameless, undefiled, separated from sinners,
and exalted above the heavens.
Unlike the other high priests,
he has no need to offer sacrifices day after day,
first for his own sins,
and then for those of the people;
this he did once for all when he offered himself.

For the law appoints as high priests
those who are subject to weakness,
but the word of the oath,
which came later than the law,
appoints a Son who has been made perfect forever.

1 Corinthians 15:45 – 50

It is written:
"The first man, Adam, became a living being";
the last Adam became a life-giving spirit.
But it is not the spiritual that is first,
but the physical, and then the spiritual.

The first was from the earth, made of dust;
the second is from heaven.

As was the one of dust, so are those who are of the dust;
and as is the one of heaven, so are those who are of heaven.

Just as we have borne the image of the one of dust,
we will also bear the image of the one of heaven.

What I am saying, brothers and sisters, is this:
flesh and blood cannot inherit the kingdom of God,
nor does the perishable inherit the imperishable.

Wisdom 18:6 – 9

The night of the deliverance from Egypt
was made known beforehand to our ancestors,
so that they might rejoice in sure knowledge of the oaths
in which they trusted.

The deliverance of the righteous
and the destruction of their enemies
were expected by your people.
For by the same means
by which you punished our enemies
you called us to yourself and glorified us.

For in secret
the holy children of good people offered sacrifices,
and with one accord agreed to the divine law,
so that the saints would share alike the same things,
both blessings and dangers;
and already they were singing the praises of the ancestors

Emphasis/Stress

Finally, a word about the most elusive of all components of vocal variety: stress, or the emphasis of certain words and phrases to communicate meaning. While not denying the importance of intelligent and sensitive emphasis, we must admit that its range is quite broad, extremely subtle, subject to regional differences and almost impossible to describe or dictate in any effective written form. The use of underlining or italics (or any such system) as a guide to the reader indicating which words to stress can do as much harm as good. Theoretically, a system could be devised that accounts for an enormous range of degree and kind of emphasis, but it would be so cumbersome as to discourage even the most eager and docile reader.

For several years, *Workbook for Lectors and Gospel Readers* has included emphasis markings to suggest to the reader which words might be stressed most effectively. Here is an example:

2 Corinthians 5:6 – 10

We *continue* to be confident.
We *know* that while we dwell in the *body*
we are away from the *Lord.*
We walk by *faith,* not by *sight.*

I repeat, we are full of *confidence,*
and would much rather be *away* from the body
and at *home* with the *Lord.*
This being *so,*
we make it our aim to *please* him
whether we are *with* him or *away* from him.

The lives of all of us are to be *revealed*
before the tribunal of *Christ*
so that each one may receive his *recompense,* good or bad,
according to his life in the *body.*

The sense of the text probably supports each choice for emphasis (the words in italics). But the experience of hearing the text would be deadly if those words were all emphasized equally, if no other words received emphasis or if the words were "punched" in the vain hope that a mechanical formula could ensure communicating the meaning — not to mention the feeling or emotion of the text.

As author of the *Workbook,* my job, in part, was to suggest words for emphasis. As my editors can attest, I acted the old curmudgeon in this matter, insisting that emphasis markings are as misleading to some as they are helpful to others. One year I won a temporary victory: The emphasis markings were reduced by two-thirds for the 1992 – 93 edition. Well, the victory was, indeed, temporary. The outcry of faithful users of the *Workbook* was so great that the next edition was again replete with emphasis markings.

Nevertheless, I remain convinced that well-formed and sensitive readers are a much better guarantee of effective stress and emphasis than any mechanical system. They are the readers who strive to communicate the text in its intellectual, emotional and aesthetic entirety — the meaning, the feeling, the beauty. They are the readers who sense that for every rule of stress there are a dozen exceptions. For example, "Never emphasize prepositions." In the selection from 2 Corinthians (above), the sense of contrast in the clause "whether we are *with* him or *away* from him" clearly justifies — even demands — emphasizing the prepositions. "Always emphasize action words (verbs)." The second and third sentences in the same selection both require emphasis on the nouns, not the verbs (except for *know*). But in the second sentence, very light emphasis on *know*, heavier emphasis of both nouns and a slightly lighter emphasis on the verb *dwell* and the preposition *away* is acceptable: "We *know* that while we dwell in the *body*, we are *away* from the *Lord*."

So where does it end? The more appropriate question, of course, is "Where does it begin?" It begins with an understanding of the text, sensitivity to how prose works and a range of vocal variety that equips the reader with nuance and subtlety. It also might begin with what we call a "good ear," another concept that has yet to be quantified in any useful way. For the minister of the Word, there are still other considerations: liturgical instinct, experience and dedication nurtured by a life of faith, and, of course, intimate familiarity with the Bible (even various translations of the Bible).

The simple truth is that an enormous range of expectations is in force in the listening process. Readers who do not meet those expectations will be difficult to understand and, ultimately, will be tuned out by the assembly. On the other hand, audiences usually have very broad tolerance for the differences that are naturally found in different speakers. Differences — not inadequacies. The reader whose articulation is "lazy" or indistinct, whose volume is insufficient, whose rate is too fast or whose pauses are awkward will lose credibility and the message will suffer.

Further exercises for practicing emphasis

Romans 8:8 – 17

Those who are in the flesh cannot please God.
But you are not in the flesh;
you are in the Spirit,
since the Spirit of God dwells in you.
Anyone who does not have the Spirit of Christ
does not belong to him.

But if Christ is in you,
though the body is dead because of sin,
the Spirit is life because of righteousness.
If the Spirit of God who raised Jesus from the dead
     dwells in you,
he who raised Christ from the dead

will give life to your mortal bodies also
through his Spirit that dwells in you.

So then, brothers and sisters,
we are debtors, not to the flesh,
to live according to the flesh —
for if you live according to the flesh, you will die;
but if by the Spirit you put to death the deeds of the body,
you will live.

For all who are led by the Spirit of God are children of God.
For you did not receive a spirit of slavery
to fall back into fear,
but you have received a spirit of adoption.
When we cry, "Abba! Father!"
it is that very Spirit bearing witness
with our spirit that we are children of God,
and if children, then heirs,
heirs of God and joint heirs with Christ —
if, in fact, we suffer with him
so that we may also be glorified with him.

Revelation 21:1 – 5a

Then I, John, saw a new heaven and a new earth;
for the first heaven and the first earth had passed away,
and the sea was no more.

And I saw the holy city, the new Jerusalem,
coming down out of heaven from God,
prepared as a bride adorned for her husband.

And I heard a loud voice from the throne saying,
"See, the home of God is among mortals.
He will dwell with them as their God;
they will be his peoples,
and God himself will be with them;
he will wipe every tear from their eyes.
Death will be no more;
mourning and crying and pain will be no more,
for the first things have passed away."
And the one who was seated on the throne said,
"See, I am making all things new."

Daniel 12:1 – 3

In the third year of King Cyrus a word was revealed
    to Daniel.
The word was true and it concerned a great conflict.

"At that time Michael, the great prince,
the protector of your people, shall arise.
There shall be a time of anguish,
such as has never occurred
since nations first came into existence.
But at that time your people shall be delivered,
everyone who is found written in the book.
Many of those who sleep
in the dust of the earth shall awake,
some to everlasting life,
and some to shame and everlasting contempt.

"Those who are wise shall shine like the brightness of the sky,
and those who lead many to righteousness,
like the stars forever and ever."

Public speaking anxiety (stage fright)

Whether you are experienced or new at this ministry, you need to deal with the number one phobia in nearly every human being: public communication anxiety, or, in more popular terms, "stage fright." If you do not experience this anxiety at all, chances are that you are not taking your ministry seriously enough or have settled for "safe" methods that render your reading too "casual," too low-key, lifeless and ineffective.

That rather stern remark brings us to the first step in dealing with stage fright: Remembering that it has a positive side. Remind yourself that such anxiety is the fear of not doing a good job or the fear of looking ridiculous. The positive side is that your fear is really the energetic desire to do well.

There is no cure for public speaking anxiety, and there is no *wish* to "cure" it. Rather, the constructive approach is to "use" it — to use the energy underlying it. The best way to use that energy is to prepare well and then proclaim the word with a high energy level. All the experts in the field of communication agree that thorough preparation is the best way to handle stage fright.

In addition, you can control the physical evidence of stage fright by breathing deeply and slowly and by becoming familiar with the liturgical environment and even enhancing it (a suitable lectern, a book which is worthy of its function, an adequate public address system, and so forth). Public performance is a skill and an art. Practice not only makes perfect (or nearly so). It also creates confidence. Therefore, seek every opportunity for public speaking experience so that your success rate is elevated. Finally, remind yourself that you share the challenge of stage fright with every dedicated performer, preacher and reader.

3 Effective Proclamation Skills

While effective communication skills are universal — that is, they are required for every public speaking situation, including proclamation of the word — there are adaptations that must be made according to the many variables of audience expectation, occasion, communicative purpose, environment and so on. Liturgical proclamation requires sensitivity to the special nature and unique elements of the liturgical setting. The ministry of reader presumes the context of an assembled worshiping community, and sacred scripture (as arranged in the lectionary for use throughout the liturgical year) is the reader's medium. Though readers are often called upon (in less than ideal circumstances) to deal with other texts (the responsorial psalm, general intercessions, announcements), the ministry of proclamation is for the purpose of proclaiming the scripture readings and the ritual dialogues that introduce and conclude them. Our considerations henceforth presume that the effective communication skills desirable in any human exchange are evident in the particular context of ritual and worship.

Ritual language

The nature of ritual language is that it is more formative than informative. Ritual language, like liturgy itself, is concerned with "doing" more than "telling." Recall the earlier discussion about "performative speech acts." We would do well to consider ritual proclamation of the word as "performative" rather than "informative." In the proclamation of the word of God, the action of God intervening in human history is continued. The words we proclaim achieve their purpose and are fulfilled in the very proclamation and hearing of them. It is necessary to insist on the special nature of ritual language in order to avoid a more pragmatic view of proclamation that would see it as instruction, information, persuasion or anything other than gratuitous praise and the continuation of God's will to redeem us in love.

Consider this: After you have been a minister of the word for several years, you will find yourself dealing over and over with familiar texts. Thus certainly your adult hearers are witnessing the proclamation of texts they have heard over and over all their lives. Ritual language is not concerned with hearing something *new*. It is concerned with expressing the familiar and hearing it *anew* each time the ritual is celebrated. The minister of the word is not a teacher, not a channel of information, not a persuader. Beginning readers have an especially difficult time redefining themselves as ritual proclaimers and not information bearers.

Read the following passage, a very familiar one, and ask yourself why it is proclaimed over and over and over again. There is no new information here, no moral instruction. There is no effort to directly persuade the hearers in any way. So why repeat it over and over? If you come up with a practical and pragmatic answer, you will miss the point. If your answer employs such terms as memorial, tradition, heritage and so forth, you are edging toward a good response. If you think that the passage is repeated because the story it tells is fulfilled in the telling of it and the inauguration of the Kingdom of God is not limited to time or space, you will proclaim it in accord with its ritual purpose.

Luke 2:1 – 14

In those days a decree went out from Emperor Augustus
that all the world should be registered.
This was the first registration
and was taken while Quirinius was governor of Syria.
All went to their own towns to be registered.
Joseph also went from the town of Nazareth in Galilee
   to Judea,
to the city of David called Bethlehem,
because he was descended from the house and family
   of David.
He went to be registered with Mary,
to whom he was engaged and who was expecting a child.

While they were there,
the time came for her to deliver her child.
And she gave birth to her firstborn son
and wrapped him in bands of cloth,
and laid him in a manger,
because there was no place for them in the inn.

In that region there were shepherds living in the fields,
keeping watch over their flock by night.
Then an angel of the Lord stood before them,
and the glory of the Lord shone around them,
and they were terrified.
But the angel said to them,
"Do not be afraid; for see—
I am bringing you good news of great joy for all the people:
to you is born this day in the city of David a Savior,
who is the Messiah, the Lord.
This will be a sign for you:
you will find a child wrapped in bands of cloth
and lying in a manger."

And suddenly there was with the angel
a multitude of the heavenly host,
praising God and saying,
"Glory to God in the highest heaven,
and on earth peace among those whom he favors!"

On the other hand, consider the following text (the first reading
on the Feast of All Saints), which is filled with extraordinary images and
information. It takes the qualities of ritual language to new heights. The
reader should approach texts such as this one for what they are: exalted
and poetic attempts to express the ineffable. They do not survive well
under the weight of staid renditions devoid of passion. (The bracketed
portion of the text has been omitted from the lectionary. The ritual num-
bering of each tribe seemed too much for the average hearer. For our
purposes here, it is included because it is an exceptional example of the
semi-hypnotic power of ritual language.)

Revelation 7:2–14

I, John, saw an angel
ascending from the rising of the sun,
having the seal of the living God,
and he called with a loud voice to the four angels
who had been given power to damage earth and sea, saying,
"Do not damage the earth or the sea or the trees,
until we have marked the servants of our God
with a seal on their foreheads."

And I heard the number of those who were sealed,
one hundred forty-four thousand,
sealed out of every tribe of the people of Israel:
[From the tribe of Judah twelve thousand sealed,
from the tribe of Reuben twelve thousand,
from the tribe of Gad twelve thousand,
from the tribe of Asher twelve thousand,
from the tribe of Naphtali twelve thousand,
from the tribe of Manasseh twelve thousand,
from the tribe of Simeon twelve thousand,
from the tribe of Levi twelve thousand,
from the tribe of Issachar twelve thousand,
from the tribe of Zebulun twelve thousand,
from the tribe of Joseph twelve thousand,
from the tribe of Benjamin twelve thousand sealed.]

After this I looked, and there was a great multitude
that no one could count, from every nation,
from all tribes and peoples and languages,
standing before the throne and before the Lamb,
robed in white, with palm branches in their hands.
They cried out in a loud voice,
"Salvation belongs to our God who is seated on the throne,
and to the Lamb!"

And all the angels stood around the throne
and around the elders and the four living creatures;
and they fell on their faces before the throne
and worshiped God, singing,
"Amen! Blessing and glory and wisdom
and thanksgiving and honor and power and might
be to our God forever and ever! Amen."

Then one of the elders addressed me,
"Who are these, robed in white,
and where have they come from?"
I said to him, "Sir, you are the one that knows."
Then he said to me,
"These are they who have come out of the great ordeal;
they have washed their robes
and made them white in the blood of the Lamb."

Liturgical dialogue

"The word of the Lord." "Thanks be to God." "A reading from the holy gospel according to Luke." "The gospel of the Lord." "Praise to you, Lord Jesus Christ." Liturgical dialogue is effective when the principle of "expected form" is observed. It loses its ritual power when it is departed from in the mistaken interest of making it literal, relevant, "warm" or informative. Thus it is important that readers be faithful to the dialogue assigned to them and not embellish or augment it in any way. To do so is to destroy the appeal of liturgy and ritual as an expected form of worship. Ritual works its long-term and subtle effect on us precisely because of its repetition and predictability. The constant search for new and potentially disarming ways to alter liturgical dialogue reveals a woeful lack of understanding of liturgy's purpose and function.

In recent years we have heard readers at pains to "refresh" liturgical dialogue by creating their own versions of it. "The word of the Lord" has seen such permutations as "And this, my brothers and sisters, is the word of the Lord." The content of the two statements is the same, perhaps, but the form, function and purpose are radically different. Aside from the fact that the congregation will be caught off guard and not be able to respond with spontaneity, the casting of the dialogue in this literal and "informative" way misses the mark in two ways: It destroys people's expectations with regard to "form," which is essential to ritual, and it "tells" us something instead of "does something."

It is only recently that the ritual form has been officially changed by the church. You may recall that the reader used to say at the end of the reading, "This is the word of the Lord." The formula was reduced to "The word of the Lord," not only in the interests of a better translation of the Latin *(Verbum Domini),* as some have asserted, but to render it more ritual (performative) and less referential (literal, informative). "This is . . ." clearly carries a feeling of the demonstrative — which explains in part the tendency some readers have had of holding the lectionary aloft while speaking the words. This practice confused things further by drawing attention to the book when the proper focus of our attention should have been on the living proclamation of the word still ringing in our ears. The fact that the shorter formula is closer to the Latin simply shows that the Latin carries the non-referential, non-demonstrative sense of a text that is more acclamation than explanation. A simple change has a subtle and important effect over time. It lessens our tendency to see the liturgy as a gathering in which we "learn" about our faith, and it intensifies our experience of the liturgy as a gathering in which we "celebrate" our faith.

Scriptural language

All of sacred scripture is written in exalted language because the writers of the scriptures were always engaged in communicating something more than just their actual words. Even what appears to be a straightforward narrative has a deeper purpose. This sense of deeper purpose explains, in part, why the gospel narratives of Matthew, Mark and Luke differ so much one from the other. The writers had a governing purpose not only in recording the events in Jesus' life but in recording them *in a certain way.* And the Gospel of John is radically different from the others. In John's account of the passion, for example, Jesus is very much in control of the situation. He is not victim; he is king and ruler. A loyal band of followers stands at the foot of his cross. In the other accounts, a mocking crowd surrounds him. John's purpose is different, so he portrays the passion of Jesus differently. Such controlling themes elevate prose far beyond the merely literal and project it into the realm of the figurative, even the poetic.

The point is that casual attempts to "translate" the translation into colloquial, informal or even "everyday" expressions is irresponsible and reveals a lack of understanding of scripture and the subtleties of its original form. More serious still is the effect of such attempts, no matter how well-intentioned or motivated: They invariably and inevitably trivialize sacred scripture. They also underestimate the sensitivities of the hearers and put the speaker in the foreground at the expense of the word of God.

Biblical literary genres

The Bible is a collection of many different kinds of literature: narratives (stories), poems, sermons, hymns, and so on. Your instinct tells you that different kinds of literature require different treatments. Trust your instincts, but avoid stereotypes. There is no reason to imitate bad Shakespearean actors when reading poetry, or Mother Goose when reading a narrative.

There is a very important reason for recognizing and respecting the different literary styles in the Bible, and it has been alluded to above. The writer's message is told in a particular way (literary form) because the writer is making a particular point or is appealing to the audience in a particular way. The choice of style is not arbitrary. A classic example, of course, is the poetry of Genesis and the accounts of creation. If we forget that the writer's purpose is to show that God is the origin and sustaining power of all that exists, we could repeat the mistake of trying to understand the poetic text literally. Knowing that there are two accounts of creation in Genesis — that do not agree with each other — should be enough to convince us that the authors were not concerned with scientific data. Poetry is usually not the style of choice for scientists.

Readers who have studied literature in high school or in college should not hesitate to approach the Bible as a collection of literature in a variety of genres. All that you studied regarding metaphor, simile, narrative, plot and denouement (resolution) is applicable. Poetic structure, word order, alliteration, onomatopoeia — these terms all apply to biblical poetry and can be quite helpful. Yes, many poetic elements such as these are lost in translation, but the better translations that exist today were done by scholars who have tried to preserve them.

The point here is the same one emphasized throughout this book: Readers often bring to the ministry of reader a wealth of experience that should be capitalized upon, not tossed aside in the mistaken notion that the literature of the Bible — and the successful proclamation of it — is so rarefied that it requires a whole new frame of reference.

Poetry

There is a great deal of poetry in the bible. The psalms, Proverbs, much of the Wisdom literature and long sections of the prophets are all written in poetic form. The challenge to the reader is to have the courage to read them as the poetry they are instead of like prose. For the most part, such adjustments in proclamation style will come naturally to the sensitive reader. There is no recommendation here to over-dramatize or become lugubrious in response to a poetic text; there is here, however, encouragement to suggest the strong emotions and feelings that are so often found in poetry.

Consider the passage below. The fourth reading at the Easter Vigil is a prophecy of the restoration of Jerusalem, the restoration of the people of Israel and the rebuilding of the temple. All these promises spoken by God are metaphors for a better time. In the context of the Easter Vigil, they are signs of the glory that will arise out of suffering and death.

Isaiah 54:5 – 14

Thus says the Lord, the God of hosts.

[Four assertions about God, four "names," and the text builds throughout. God in heaven, in Israel, IN THE ENTIRE WORLD!]

Your Maker is your husband,
the LORD of hosts is his name;

the Holy One of Israel is your Redeemer,
the God of the whole earth he is called.

[The gentler images of marital love require a gentler tone. Pity and compassion.]

For the LORD has called you
like a wife forsaken and grieved in spirit,
like the wife of a man's youth when she is cast off,
says your God.

[A series of contrasts follows, very effective when the emphasis is well-placed. "I abandoned . . . BUT . . . I hid . . . BUT . . .]

For a brief moment I abandoned you,
but with great compassion I will gather you.
In overflowing wrath for a moment
I hid my face from you,
but with everlasting love I will have compassion on you,
says the LORD, your Redeemer.

[The following two sentences seem at first to be more narrative than poetic, but notice that the introduction of Noah is simply for purposes of comparison. An allusion to God's fidelity in the past strengthens the promise of fidelity being made now. Likewise, the stability of the mountains and hills is nothing compared to the dependability of God's promises.]

This is like the days of Noah to me:
Just as I swore that the waters of Noah
would never again go over the earth,
so I have sworn that I will not be angry with you
and will not rebuke you.
For the mountains may depart and the hills be removed,
but my steadfast love shall not depart from you,
and my covenant of peace shall not be removed,
says the LORD, who has compassion on you.

[The word "O" emphasizes the feeling of compassion. The series of precious stones as metaphors for restoration is particularly exalted.]

O afflicted one, storm-tossed, and not comforted,
I am about to set your stones in antimony,
and lay your foundations with sapphires.
I will make your pinnacles of rubies,
your gates of jewels,
and all your wall of precious stones.

[Two parallel constructions — children the subject of the first, freedom from oppression the subject of the second — surround a straightforward promise: "In righteousness. . . ."]

All your children shall be taught by the LORD,
and great shall be the prosperity of your children.
In righteousness you shall be established;

you shall be far from oppression, for you shall not fear;
and from terror, for it shall not come near you.

Narrative

Here is a passage in narrative form. We have dealt with this text before in the discussion on effective pausing. Notice that it is, in effect, a short story, the story of Saul's first difficulties in overcoming his reputation as a persecutor of the fledgling church before he becomes "Paul, apostle to the Gentiles." Narrative can move between events and commentary on those events quite easily. That's what happens here. In the narratives of the gospels, and especially in the passion of Jesus, there is an even more straightforward telling of events but always with an underlying tone or purpose. What is the purpose of recording the events in the reading that follows here? Is it to record the change in how Saul/Paul is received? Is it to provide an opportunity for sharing the story of Saul's conversion ("he had seen the Lord")? Is it to remind the reader of the rejection suffered by the good news ("attempting to kill him")? Yes, it is all these things, but the summary paragraph at the end is probably our best guide. The vicissitudes involved in spreading the good news cannot suppress it; the believers are growing in number and in strength. In every narrative there is usually a controlling idea or theme that explains its presence. Try to find that theme and formulate it in your own words. Then your proclamation of the narrative will be more cohesive and intelligible and will tie events together under the guiding theme.

Acts 9:26 – 31

When Saul had come to Jerusalem,
he attempted to join the disciples;
and they were all afraid of him,
for they did not believe that he was a disciple.
But Barnabas took him,
brought him to the apostles,
and described for them how on the road
    he had seen the Lord,
who had spoken to him,
and how in Damascus he had spoken boldly
    in the name of Jesus.

So Saul went in and out among them in Jerusalem,
speaking boldly in the name of the Lord.
He spoke and argued with the Hellenists;

but they were attempting to kill him.
When the believers learned of it,
they brought him down to Caesarea and sent him off
    to Tarsus.

Meanwhile the church throughout Judea, Galilee, and Samaria
had peace and was built up.
Living in the fear of the Lord
and in the comfort of the Holy Spirit,
it increased in numbers.

Exercise for narration

For sheer narrative power, it is difficult to do better than Luke's story of
the disciples on the road to Emmaus. It is a brief short story fraught with
strong emotion, sudden revelation and renewed faith. Read this story
with all the fervor you can, and you will have improved your narrative
skills almost inevitably.

Luke 24:13 – 35

On the first day of the week,
two of the disciples were going to a village called Emmaus,
about seven miles from Jerusalem,
and talking with each other
about all these things that had happened.
While they were talking and discussing,
Jesus himself came near and went with them,
but their eyes were kept from recognizing him.

And Jesus said to them,
"What are you discussing with each other
    while you walk along?"
They stood still, looking sad.
Then one of them, whose name was Cleopas, answered him,
"Are you the only stranger in Jerusalem
who does not know the things
that have taken place there in these days?"

Jesus asked them, "What things?"
They replied, "The things about Jesus of Nazareth,
who was a prophet mighty in deed and word
before God and all the people,
and how our chief priests and leaders handed him over

to be condemned to death and crucified him.
But we had hoped that he was the one to redeem Israel.
Yes, and besides all this,
it is now the third day since these things took place.
Moreover, some women of our group astounded us.
They were at the tomb early this morning,
and when they did not find his body there,
they came back
and told us that they had indeed seen a vision of angels
who said that he was alive.
Some of those who were with us went to the tomb
and found it just as the women had said;
but they did not see Jesus."

Then Jesus said to them,
"Oh, how foolish you are,
and how slow of heart
to believe all that the prophets have declared!
Was it not necessary that the Messiah should suffer
    these things
and then enter into his glory?"

Then beginning with Moses and all the prophets,
Jesus interpreted to them
the things about himself in all the scriptures.
As they came near the village to which they were going,
Jesus walked ahead as if he were going on.
But they urged him strongly, saying,
"Stay with us, because it is almost evening
and the day is now nearly over."
So he went in to stay with them.

When he was at the table with them,
he took bread, blessed and broke it,
and gave it to them.
Then their eyes were opened, and they recognized Jesus;
and he vanished from their sight.

The two disciples said to each other,
"Were not our hearts burning within us
while he was talking to us on the road,
while he was opening the scriptures to us?"

That same hour they got up and returned to Jerusalem;
and they found the eleven and their companions
    gathered together.
These were saying,
"The Lord has risen indeed, and he has appeared to Simon!"

Then the two disciples told what had happened on the road,
and how the Lord had been made known to them
in the breaking of the bread.

Discourse

In discourse, an argument is presented, an explanation is offered, or the writer simply draws out the implications of an event or a divine action. Here Paul is explaining that, although our redemption has been accomplished in Christ, it is not yet fully realized. It is what some have called the great irony of Christian life — the "already, but not yet" experience. We've already been saved, but we are still being saved, and the full experience of our salvation lies in the future. Thus the natural condition for believers is one of hope.

Paul extends the longing for the fullness of salvation to the earth itself; all creation (even inanimate creation) is incomplete until the fullness of redemption and re-creation is complete. The earth itself is "hoping" for that day of full restoration, that day when God and creation will be in perfect harmony as in the days before Adam's sin. That sin subjected everything to futility; Jesus' death and resurrection has liberated everything in hope!

Discourse is, in some ways, the most difficult literary genre to proclaim and is sometimes even more difficult to hear. It requires more study, a deeper analysis of its prose structure and a very careful rendering. Very often a theological kind of logic is used in discourse — a logic more typical of the Middle Eastern mentality than our own syllogistic kind of argumentation. The reader will have to surrender a tendency to grasp irritably for hard facts in biblical discourse. But the development of the argument is cogent, given the writer's method and intention.

Romans 8:18 – 23

I consider that the sufferings of this present time
are not worth comparing with the glory
about to be revealed to us.
For the creation waits with eager longing

for the revealing of the children of God;
for the creation was subjected to futility,
not of its own will
but by the will of the one who subjected it,
in hope that the creation itself
will be set free from its bondage to decay
and will obtain the freedom of the glory
    of the children of God.

We know that the whole creation
has been groaning in labor pains until now;
and not only the creation,
but we ourselves, who have the first fruits of the Spirit,
groan inwardly while we wait for adoption,
the redemption of our bodies.

Exercise for discourse

In the book of Deuteronomy, Moses engages in a discourse with the Israelites, expounding on the duties and obligations that accompany the blessing of being God's Chosen People. Parts of the text are proclaimed on the Ninth Sunday in Ordinary Time (Year A). Though different from Paul's discourse presented earlier, it nevertheless has the ring of reasoned argument. Think of it as a persuasion speech.

Deuteronomy 10:12 – 13, 11:18 – 28

Moses spoke to the people and said:
"So now, O Israel,
what does the LORD your God require of you?
Only to fear the LORD your God,
to walk in all his ways, to love him,
to serve the LORD your God
with all your heart and with all your soul,
and to keep the commandments of the LORD your God
and his decrees that I am commanding you today,
for your own well-being.

"You shall put these words of mine in your heart and soul,
and you shall bind them as a sign on your hand,
and fix them as an emblem on your forehead.
Teach them to your children, talking about them
when you are at home and when you are away,
when you lie down and when you rise.

"Write them on the doorposts of your house
 and on your gates,
so that your days and the days of your children
may be multiplied in the land
that the LORD swore to your ancestors to give them,
as long as the heavens are above the earth.

"If you will diligently observe this entire commandment
that I am commanding you,
loving the LORD your God, walking in all his ways,
and holding fast to him,
then the LORD will drive out all these nations before you,
and you will dispossess nations larger and mightier
 than yourselves.
Every place on which you set foot shall be yours;
your territory shall extend
from the wilderness to the Lebanon and from the River,
the river Euphrates, to the Western Sea.
No one will be able to stand against you;
the LORD your God will put the fear and dread of you
on all the land on which you set foot, as he promised you.

"See, I am setting before you today a blessing and a curse:
the blessing,
if you obey the commandments of the LORD your God
that I am commanding you today;
and the curse,
if you do not obey the commandments of the LORD your God,
but turn from the way that I am commanding you today,
to follow other gods that you have not known.

Parables

The word "parable" has a revealing etymology: It is rooted in the notion of "one thing laid alongside another for comparison" — not a bad way to think of parable as a literary form. The important thing to remember is that comparison, not exact similarity or a perfect match, is the point. Therefore, parables often have what appear to be inconsistencies, inequalities, and contradictions within them.

The parable that follows was chosen because it seems to contain a contradiction. The first time most people hear it, they no doubt react in their minds with something like this: "Wait a minute! I agree with the guy who registered the complaint. This is a very unfair way of going about things!" Precisely. And now we've come to the heart of what "parable" means. To make the answer too simplistic, "God's ways are different from our ways." As insufficient as that explanation may seem, it is the underlying point of the parable: God's generosity is so outrageously different from our own that we need to change our way of thinking if we want to be radically God-like.

Matthew 20:1 – 16

"For the kingdom of heaven is like a landowner
who went out early in the morning
to hire laborers for his vineyard.

"After agreeing with the laborers for the usual daily wage,
he sent them into his vineyard.
When he went out about nine o'clock,
he saw others standing idle in the marketplace;
and he said to them,
'You also go into the vineyard,
and I will pay you whatever is right.'
So they went.

"When he went out again about noon and about three o'clock,
he did the same.
And about five o'clock he went out and found others
standing around;
and he said to them,
'Why are you standing here idle all day?'
They said to him,
'Because no one has hired us.'
He said to them,
'You also go into the vineyard.'

"When evening came,
the owner of the vineyard said to his manager,
'Call the laborers and give them their pay,
beginning with the last and then going to the first.'
When those hired about five o'clock came,
each of them received the usual daily wage.
Now when the first came,
they thought they would receive more;
but each of them also received the usual daily wage.
And when they received it,
they grumbled against the landowner, saying,

'These last worked only one hour,
and you have made them equal to us
who have borne the burden of the day
    and the scorching heat.'
But he replied to one of them,
'Friend, I am doing you no wrong;
did you not agree with me for the usual daily wage?
Take what belongs to you and go;
I choose to give to this last the same as I give to you.
Am I not allowed to do what I choose
with what belongs to me?
Or are you envious because I am generous?'

"So the last will be first,
and the first will be last."

Some parables are more like extended metaphors. The comparison is developed without narrative. The parables of the kingdom of God are good examples. The kingdom of God is like a dragnet, like a mustard seed, and so forth. These brief nuggets of insight into the nature of the kingdom are pictures worth a thousand words. Exploit them.

Matthew 13:31 – 33

Jesus put before them another parable:
"The kingdom of heaven is like a mustard seed
that someone took and sowed in his field;
it is the smallest of all the seeds,
but when it has grown
it is the greatest of shrubs and becomes a tree,
so that the birds of the air come and make nests
    in its branches."

He told them another parable:
"The kingdom of heaven is like yeast
that a woman took and mixed in with three measures of flour
until all of it was leavened."

4 *The Lectionary*

Your ministry as reader centers on the church's arrangement of Bible readings into a complex volume still subject to revision and refinement — the lectionary (from the Latin word *lectio,* which means reading). When the Second Vatican Council insisted that the riches of sacred scripture be opened up more lavishly for the faithful, we had lived for many years with a set of readings that were the same each year and for every day of the year. The new lectionary nearly triples our exposure to the Bible during liturgical worship with a collection of readings covering a three-year cycle for the Sunday liturgy and a two-year cycle for liturgies celebrated on weekdays.

The new lectionary is still in transition, and we will no doubt continue to see improvements in the selection of scriptural texts (and in the way they are edited for public proclamation) for several more years to come. We will also see improved translations in the future that take into consideration such issues as inclusive language. Nevertheless, the lectionary in its current state is a vast improvement over the old system. Its arrangement is complex only in the sense that it takes the beginner some time to understand its structure and flexibility. One who serves as reader at the liturgy must have a working relationship with the lectionary as well as an understanding of the aims and purposes that guided those who assembled it.

The most obvious feature of the lectionary is its organization in accord with the liturgical calendar. There is a cycle of Sundays and feasts that begins with the liturgical seasons of Advent and Christmas and includes Lent, Easter and Pentecost. Between Christmas and Lent, and again between Pentecost and Advent, is Ordinary Time. The word "ordinary" here has nothing to do with being "plain" or "common." The root word is "ordinal" (referring to numbers) and indicates that Ordinary Time is composed of consecutively numbered Sundays. Nevertheless, the name "Ordinary Time" has different connotations for most people, and we ought to come up with a better one. There is nothing ordinary about it except that it deals, for the most part, with aspects of our faith that are perhaps less dramatic than those of the other seasons. One of my professors used to call Ordinary Time "No Particular Reason Season," but his intention in doing so was to point out the irony in calling any part of the liturgical year "ordinary," regardless of the true origin of the word.

The liturgical year: structure and purpose

The liturgical year we celebrate today has a long and fascinating history. The round of seasons and feasts was not devised all at once but developed over many centuries and under many influences. Many celebrations in the Christian calendar find their inspiration and origins in the religious experience and tradition of the Jews, our forebears in faith. The Jewish feast of Passover, as all Christians know, has become our Easter. The point is that the liturgical cycle of seasons and feast days we now observe has a long and complex history that owes much to pre-Christian, sometimes even pagan, influences. It is important to view the liturgical year as a living and evolving way of expressing our faith experience. It is subject to change and growth, just as our faith is.

If we were to search for the most fundamentally stable element in the liturgical year — the event or celebration upon which the entire cycle is based — we would not find it in the yearly round of seasons (Advent, Christmas, Lent, Easter, Pentecost). No, we would find it in the Sabbath celebration, the day set aside for the Lord, which for Christians is the Sunday assembly, the weekly gathering for the purpose of celebrating the eucharist. It is the Sunday gathering of believers that antedates every season and every feast, except, of course, Easter, with which the Sunday celebration is always identified. The entire liturgical year is founded on the observance of this Lord's Day, and the entire liturgical year is encompassed by every Sunday eucharist. "Christ has died, Christ is risen, Christ will come again." Salvation history in ten words! One of the most important reforms prompted by the Second Vatican Council was the re-establishment of Sundays as the focal points of the liturgical year. Only rarely does a particular feast of great significance supplant a Sunday upon which it happens to occur.

The seasons of the church year surround the central mysteries of our faith, providing a time of preparation for their celebration, giving them emphasis and enabling us to concentrate on the fullness of their significance. Each has its own particular character and spirit, arising from the event in salvation history that gave rise to it as well as our own experience of it in our worshiping communities. And, of course, the biblical readings chosen for the Sundays and weekdays within a given season reflect that character and spirit.

In order to abide by the Second Vatican Council's wish that more biblical texts be proclaimed at the liturgy, two major changes were made. The Sunday liturgy of the word was expanded from two readings (epistle and gospel) to include an additional selection, what we know now as the first reading. It is almost always from the Hebrew Scriptures (the Old Testament) and is chosen with the gospel of the day in mind. The second reading is taken from New Testament books other than the gospels; no particular relationship to the other readings guides its choice. When the liturgical cycle of readings was expanded from one year to three (Years A, B, C), gospel readings from the three synoptics, Matthew, Mark and Luke, were assigned respectively. These three evangelists wrote a kind of "synopsis" of Jesus' life and ministry, not a summary or outline (in the sense of an abridgment) but a more or less sequential narrative. The Gospel of John, very different in character and purpose from the synoptics, fills in occasionally but is primarily reserved for the Easter season in all three years.

A brief look at the liturgical seasons and the biblical sources for the readings that are proclaimed during each one can serve as a cursory look at the structure of the lectionary. However, only attentive and prolonged use of the lectionary will reveal both its genius and its need for further revision and fine tuning. Notice also in the following discussion that the seasons do not begin or end abruptly; rather, they segue one into the next so that the effect of a seamless garment is maintained.

Reviewing the structure of the Advent readings in some detail will give you a general idea of how the themes of a season are supported and developed by the choice of scriptural readings over the entire three-year liturgical cycle. One of the most remarkable achievements of the expanded lectionary is that we gain a much richer view of the mysteries of our faith — simply because we hear from so many different Bible authors who each have a particular emphasis or insight to offer.

Advent and Christmas/Epiphany: the comings of the Lord

It is not difficult to remember at the beginning of each new liturgical year that Advent is concerned with more than the birth of Jesus in Bethlehem 2000 years ago. The last few Sundays in Ordinary Time are full of references to the "end time," the coming of Christ in glory at the end of the world. The last Sunday in Ordinary Time is celebrated as the solemnity of Christ the King. Thus we are also reminded at the beginning of the new liturgical year that each season emerges from the preceding one and leads us into the next.

The first reading during Advent is always from the prophets who foretell the restoration of Israel and, by Christian application, the coming of the promised Messiah. There is one exception: On the Fourth Sunday of Advent in Year B the text of the first reading is taken from the Second Book of Samuel. But even in this instance, God's promises to David are the subject; Jesus is born of the house of David. Isaiah holds preeminence among the "advent prophets" and gives us seven of the twelve first readings in the three-year cycle (A, B, C).

The second reading is chosen from Romans and James in Year A; 1 Corinthians, 2 Peter, 1 Thessalonians and Romans in Year B; 1 Thessalonians, Philemon and Hebrews in Year C. The selections are all chosen for their concern with the imminent coming of the Lord, the guaranteed accomplishment of salvation by the Lord, "the day of the Lord" and patient endurance in hope — all themes which make the "second coming" of Jesus vividly present in the Advent liturgies.

The gospel readings during Advent embrace both the Lord's coming in time and at the end of time, beginning with the latter. Matthew (Year A), Mark (Year B) and Luke (Year C) give us Jesus' own words about the coming of the Son of Man at the end of time. On the second Sunday of Advent, each gives us his own account of John the Baptist, contemporary and precursor of the Messiah. On the third Sunday, we continue to hear of John the Baptist, but the Gospel of John is used in Year B because Mark's gospel is so brief on the subject.

On the fourth and last Sunday of Advent we move closer to the Christmas theme. In years A and B we hear the accounts of the annunciation, found in Matthew and in Luke. The angel Gabriel appears to Mary with the announcement that she will be the mother of Jesus. Luke must fill in for Mark in Year B because Mark does not deal with the birth or infancy of Jesus. And we hear again from Luke in Year C (the year proper to him) when he recounts the story of Mary's visit to her cousin Elizabeth.

The season of Advent has brought us to the very threshold of the Christmas feast, which is then revealed in its several aspects through the related celebrations of Holy Family, Mother of God (New Year's Day), Epiphany, and finally, the Baptism of the Lord, which serves to inaugurate Ordinary Time — as, indeed, the historical event itself signaled the inauguration of Jesus' public ministry and the new kingdom of God upon earth.

We see how the seasons of Advent and Christmas/Epiphany move seamlessly into Ordinary Time, with the feast of the Lord's baptism serving as the conclusion of one and the introduction of the other. It is not difficult to see how the Lord's baptism inaugurates the new season, but how is it related to the Advent/Christmas celebration? The answer to this question reveals another aspect of the liturgical year: It is not based on historical events or on the sequential passage of time alone. Rather, there is a sacramental and theological basis for the liturgical year that transcends time and space. The ultimate meaning of Advent, Christmas and Epiphany is that the long-awaited Messiah has at last come and is the manifestation of God on earth. The word "epiphany" means "manifestation," or "showing forth." The baptism of Jesus, with its accompanying signs of the dove and the voice from heaven ("This is my beloved Son!") has always been celebrated in close association with the "epiphanies" of the Lord's coming in time. This is a view made explicit in an ancient text we find in the Liturgy of the Hours on the feast of the Epiphany: "We celebrate three miracles today. Today the three Magi offered gifts to the infant king in the manger. Today Jesus turned water into wine at the wedding feast of Cana. Today Christ was baptized in the Jordan by John." (In Year C, Luke's story of the wedding feast at Cana is heard on the Second Sunday in Ordinary Time.) Though these three events took place at different points in historical time, in the sacramental time of the liturgical year they are all manifestations of God's presence upon the earth in a new and wonderful way. From a sacramental point of view, they are celebrated as one.

Ordinary Time I: the inauguration of the Kingdom

The First Sunday in Ordinary Time is the feast of the Lord's baptism (celebrated sometime within the second week of January). The Sundays that follow take us up to Ash Wednesday and the beginning of Lent. The number of Sundays in this first part of Ordinary Time depends on the date of Easter, which of course determines the date of Ash Wednesday, when the forty days of Lent begin. Easter is celebrated on the first Sunday after the first full moon after the vernal equinox (the day every spring when night and day are of nearly equal length). Now we see still another influence on our liturgical calendar: the lunar calendar and the annual celebration of Passover.

The Sundays in Ordinary Time (both before and after Lent, Easter and Pentecost) are characterized by gospel readings (Matthew in Year A, Mark in Year B, Luke in Year C) that follow Jesus through his public life and ministry. The narratives dealing with his passion, death and resurrection and the coming of the Holy Spirit are read during Lent and through Easter and Pentecost. The Gospel of John appears throughout the Easter season.

The first reading (from the Hebrew Scriptures) is chosen with some relationship to the gospel in mind. The second reading is from a New Testament book other than one of the gospels, and large sections of them are read more or less consecutively.

Throughout the long season of Ordinary Time (both before and after the Lent/Easter season) we can discern in the scripture readings a well-crafted and orderly progression toward the fulfillment of the kingdom in the final days, when Jesus the Son of God will return in majesty as Christ the King.

During Ordinary Time it perhaps becomes more apparent that the plan of the lectionary is not without its compromises. In the way it deals with passages from the Hebrew Scriptures, the lectionary often gives the impression that they are to be understood primarily, perhaps only, in light of the gospel readings they were chosen to "match." The fact is, the Old Testament is a part of our salvation history that can stand on its own without having to be interpreted only as a prefiguring of New Testament events. With such considerations in mind, the lectionary will no doubt continue to undergo revisions and improvements; nevertheless, it merits very careful study and appreciation by the minister of the word.

Lent and the Sacred Triduum: the cost of discipleship

With Ash Wednesday, the forty days of Lent begin and bring us to the center of the Christian experience: the paschal mystery, the death and resurrection of the Lord. We might say that all the New Testament readings during this season concern themselves with what it takes to be a follower of Jesus — that is, the cost of discipleship. The Old Testament readings are particularly rich and challenging, taking us back to the very beginnings of salvation history with the creation of humankind in Genesis, the establishment of the covenant with Abraham and the sojourn of the chosen people through forty years of exile. Lent has been described in many ways, perhaps best among them as a time for "getting back to basics."

Holy Week, beginning with Palm Sunday, is replete with texts that summon up the strongest of emotions. The focus narrows sharply during the Triduum to the very last hours of Jesus' ministry and his suffering, death and burial. The long Easter Vigil, with its seven readings, is a feast of God's word building toward the triumphal shout of "Alleluia! The tomb is empty!"

Easter and Pentecost: the New Order

And that cry continues for forty-nine days (a week of weeks) until the fullness of the Easter mystery is achieved in the coming of the Holy Spirit on the fiftieth day (Pentecost). The seven Sundays of Eastertime and the feast of Pentecost are unique in the lectionary. The first reading (at all other times from the Hebrew Scriptures) is selected from the Acts of the Apostles, the record of the earliest days of the new Christian community, and the gospel text is always from John, the evangelist whose view of the Lord is the most soaring and transcendent.

Ordinary Time II: the growth of the Kingdom

After the Ascension, after the coming of the Holy Spirit, the fledgling Christian community is charged with spreading the good news throughout the world. And the lectionary returns to where we left off in Jesus' ministry in the first part of Ordinary Time, witnessing the inexorable growth of the newly established kingdom through his words and deeds.

We know that the sacramental cycle of another year of grace is coming to a close when we begin to hear Jesus speak once again, toward the end of his public life, of the great day to come, when the Son of Man will return in glory. Again, even as we find ourselves contemplating that awesome final coming, we are reminded of that strikingly different "first advent" in a manger in Bethlehem.

We do well to think of the liturgical year as a cycle, not a circle. We do not simply repeat ourselves year after year in celebrating the liturgical year. Each time we complete the cycle we are on a higher plane than when we began it. We have mounted higher and moved ever closer to that day when seasons and time will be no more. There can be no more vivid reminder that we are a pilgrim people, on the way, than to enter wholeheartedly into the church's year of grace.

5 Three Years, Three Gospels, Three Views

In the lectionary we have a three-year cycle of readings guided by the three synoptic gospel narratives used in sequence over that cycle. In other words, in Year A Matthew guides us through the annual round of liturgical celebrations; then Mark does the same in Year B; and then Luke shows us the way through Year C. Once we appreciate the particular theology and view of Jesus that each evangelist provides in his narrative, we begin to see the degree to which our experience of God's word is enriched by such a plan. Over the course of the three years we find a richness that enables us to reflect meditatively upon the life of Jesus and to shape our own lives according to the paschal mystery.

The Gospel of John does not receive short shrift in this arrangement. It appears during the Easter season in all three years of the cycle and often fills in at other times, most often for Mark, whose gospel is the shortest of the four.

The gospel writers are best understood according to scholars' perception that they construct their texts on three different levels. The first level is their purpose for writing, their intention to reveal Jesus to their readers in a certain way and for a certain reason. Like any author, their view of their subject is determined by their view of the world. It is primarily this level that accounts for different emphases and a variety of insights into the person, life and ministry of Jesus. The second level of the gospel texts is the tradition regarding Jesus as it had been held and developed by the earliest believers, inherited by the gospel writers and proclaimed by their contemporaries. And the third level is the actual historical and authenticated deeds and words performed and spoken by Jesus. From a chronological point of view, we might reverse the order: authenticated historical events, the traditions and beliefs developing from those events and the particular interpretation of those traditions by the writer for his own immediate purpose.

It is, obviously, at the first level of each gospel narrative (Matthew's, Mark's, Luke's) that we find three different ways of understanding the identity, life and ministry of Jesus. Quite a number of stories appear in each of the three synoptic gospels, yet the stories are different in each narrative. The communities in which the gospel writers themselves lived experienced the risen Jesus in different ways, which accounts for the differences in the stories. Knowing this invites us, as believers and as ministers of the word of God, to travel further into the mystery of God as it was revealed in Jesus of Nazareth. Like the members of those early communities, we are expected to discover the risen Jesus in our communities. By the proclamation of the scriptures, our own experience of Jesus, indeed our faith in general, is enriched. Needless to say, such enrichment will find its way into our proclamation. The brief sketches below are far from exhaustive. The hope is that they will lead the minister of the word into further study — and a new discovery of the joy of knowledgeable proclamation.

Year A and the Gospel of Matthew

Matthew's gospel begins with a genealogy of Jesus that presents him as a descendant of a long line. Immediately we are confronted with one of Matthew's convictions about Jesus: He is the fulfillment of Jewish history. He is the Son of David, a new Solomon, wisdom incarnate. To understand Jesus fully, one must return to the Hebrew scriptures and study carefully all the promises that are fulfilled in him.

The kingdom that Jesus has come to establish is actually a restoration of the covenant made long ago with Israel. Jesus himself proclaims, "I have come not to destroy the law and the prophets, but to bring them to perfection." It is a kingdom of justice, which for Matthew means a kingdom in which obedience to God's law is the sign of membership. In supporting the commandments of old, Jesus is revealed by Matthew as a second Moses, a great lawgiver, who does not abolish the commandments but teaches and explicates them. Love of God and love of neighbor are the greatest commandments — as, indeed, they always have been. The nature of a kingdom typified by love and obedience is revealed over and over, and in many different ways, in this gospel narrative replete with "parables of the kingdom." The kingdom is like a mustard seed, like a dragnet. Matthew's masterpiece, the Sermon on the Mount, is meant to remind us of that other great mountain, Sinai, where

God was revealed and delivered the ten commandants into the hands of Moses.

"You are Peter, and upon this rock I will build my church." In the words of Jesus, the community of followers emerges only in Matthew as "church." Nowhere else in the gospels do we find the Greek word *ekklesia,* and it appears again in the context of a discussion on how to deal with sinners. The church community is the restored "people of God," awaiting the full and final revelation of Jesus as the Son of God at the end of the world.

Year B and the Gospel of Mark

Three major themes appear in Mark's gospel: concern with the identity and origin of Jesus, the nature of the kingdom of God and the characteristics of genuine discipleship. Mark also uses a technique that both reveals and withholds at the same time. There is an air of "seeing but not fully understanding" throughout the text that mirrors our own faith experience.

Who is this mysterious person? This question dominates the first half of Mark's gospel. The question is answered at the exact middle of the sixteen-chapter narrative. Peter's resounding cry, "You are the Messiah!" comes in the eighth chapter. It is not a complete answer, of course, because there is no way to know precisely who Jesus is until after the resurrection. Meanwhile, Mark shows us a teacher with a new kind of authority, a wonder-worker, teacher and healer. He shows us someone who bears the seal of God's approval, who is the fulfillment of the ancient promises of a Messiah — though different from what his contemporaries expected.

What is the kingdom of God? This question too is answered only in part. The parables about the kingdom prompt us toward an intuitive, not an analytical, understanding. Any genuine experience of faith is mirrored in Mark's "partly revealed/partly concealed" reign of God. Our belief is centered on a mystery, and Mark's gospel never ceases to remind us of that.

What is true discipleship? The answer to this question is deceptively simple. True discipleship consists in imitating Jesus. But as Mark shows us so vividly, it is neither easily embraced nor easily sustained. Again and again, Jesus' disciples are incapable of understanding the true nature — and above all the true cost — of discipleship. Their initial response to the call is both dramatic and admirable, but this is before they begin to learn what it truly involves. The second half of the gospel shows us relentless infidelity. And how could it be otherwise — before the resurrection?

In its original form, the Gospel of Mark ends at the empty tomb. The resurrection narrative and post-resurrection stories were added later. Was this another way for Mark to assert that it is our belief, our faith — not knowledge or hard evidence — that makes us followers of Jesus?

Year C and the Gospel of Luke

Luke is an elegant writer, a patrician sounding a note of gentle love and quiet wisdom in every word. The very structure of Luke's gospel reveals much about his view of discipleship and about the character of the master. Luke begins his narrative in the temple, where Zachary, the father of John the Baptist, is serving as priest. He ends the story with these words following the ascension of Jesus into heaven: "The disciples returned to Jerusalem with great joy, where they were continually in the temple praising God." Between these two images of praise and prayer there are many instances in Luke that assert the importance of both prayer and praise in the life of the Christian. It is Luke who gives us the *Benedictus* and the *Magnificat,* the two canticles that frame the church's day of prayer even to this day.

The reconstitution of Israel is another theme in Luke. The Chosen People (Israel) have been dispersed and scattered by their enemies and their own sins. But they will be brought back through the inexorable promise of God's plan to redeem the world. The "promise of restoration" is a constant in Luke.

The universality of God's love, excluding no one but including particularly the unloved, is one of the most striking of Luke's motifs. We hear it first very early in his narrative when he uses Isaiah to herald the coming redeemer but includes more of Isaiah's text than either Mark or Matthew: Luke includes "All flesh shall see the salvation of our God." The role of women in Luke is particularly notable, given society's view of their position in his day. It is to humble shepherds that the angels first proclaim the birth of the Lord. And it is Jesus himself who says, "I have come to call sinners, not the righteous, to repentance."

Jesus often appears in Luke in the context of a meal. Whenever that scene presents itself we know that Luke is hinting at its wider significance: the eternal banquet to which the lowly and the poor have a special invitation. Jesus himself is portrayed in Luke as the lowliest of the low, meek and humble of heart, identified completely with the poor.

Mary's canticle in response to Elizabeth's greeting (1:52–55) concludes with words that encompass much of Luke's view:

> "He has brought down the powerful from their thrones,
> and lifted up the lowly;
> he has filled the hungry with good things,
> and sent the rich away empty.
> He has helped his servant Israel,
> in remembrance of his mercy,
> according to the promise he made to our ancestors,
> to Abraham and to his descendants forever."

Through Years A, B and C with the gospel writers

One way to get an overview and a sense of direction in any given liturgical year is to construct charts like the ones that follow for Matthew, Mark and Luke in Years A, B and C, respectively. The headings are simply one way to recapitulate the major themes in each gospel writer. The snippets of scripture are not altogether arbitrary, since they are an attempt to grasp the "controlling idea or theme" in each gospel reading. The advantage of such a bird's eye view is that one begins to see patterns and directions. At the very least, the effort and study that goes into creating charts like these results in a review of the plan of the lectionary and an overview of each gospel writer's way of revealing the Lord's life and ministry.

Year A, Matthew's gospel

Advent – Christmas

Fulfillment of the End

1 Advent	Matthew 24:37–44	The Son of Man is coming!

Fulfillment of the Beginning

2 Advent	Matthew 3:1–12	The reign of God is at hand!
3 Advent	Matthew 11:2–11	Are you "He who is to come"?
4 Advent	Matthew 1:18–24	All this happened to fulfill . . .
Christmas Vigil	Matthew 1:1–25	A family record
Christmas	Luke 2:1–14	*There were shepherds keeping watch*
Holy Family	Matthew 2:13–15,19–23	To fulfill what the Lord had said
Mother of God	Luke 2:16–21	*Mary treasured these things*
Epiphany	Matthew 2:1–12	Here is what the prophet has written
Baptism of the Lord	Matthew 3:13–17	We would fulfill all of God's demands

Ordinary Time I

The Kingdom Is at Hand

2 Ordinary Time	John 1:29–34	*This is God's Chosen One!*
3 Ordinary Time	Matthew 4:12–23	The kingdom of heaven is at hand

Fulfilling the Law and the Prophets

4 Ordinary Time	Matthew 5:1–12	On the mountainside: Blest are those . . .
5 Ordinary Time	Matthew 5:13–16	You are the light of the world
6 Ordinary Time	Matthew 5:17–37	I have come not to abolish, but to fulfill
7 Ordinary Time	Matthew 5:38–48	My command to you is . . .
8 Ordinary Time	Matthew 6:24–34	Seek first the kingdom of God
9 Ordinary Time	Matthew 7:21–27	Jesus went up the mountain
10 Ordinary Time	Matthew 9:9–13	I have come to call sinners

Lent

Fulfilling the Scriptures

1 Lent	Matthew 4:1–11	If you are the Son of God . . .
2 Lent	Matthew 17:1–9	Until the Son of Man rises from the dead
3 Lent	John 4:5–42	*Could this not be the Messiah?*
4 Lent	John 9:1–41	*Do you believe in the Son of Man?*
5 Lent	John 11:1–45	*The Son of God will be glorified!*
Passion Sunday	Matthew 21:1–11	God save the Son of David!
	Matthew 26:14 — 27:66	All this happened to fulfill the scriptures

| Holy Thursday | John 13:1–15 | *As I have done, so you must do* |
| Good Friday | John 18:1—19:42 | *King of the Jews* |

Easter

Exactly as He Said

Easter Vigil	Matthew 28:1–10	He has been raised, exactly as he said
Easter Morning	John 20:1–9	*John saw and believed*
Easter Evening	Luke 24:13–35	*Were not our hearts burning inside us?*
2 Easter	John 20:19–31	*To help you believe that Jesus is the Messiah*
3 Easter	Luke 24:13–35	*He explained the scriptures to us*
4 Easter	John 10:1–10	*That they may have life to the full*
5 Easter	John 14:1–12	*From darkness into his marvelous light*
6 Easter	John 14:15–21	*I will not leave you orphaned*
7 Easter	John 17:1–11	*These have known that I came from you*
Pentecost	John 20:19–23	*Receive the Holy Spirit*

Ordinary Time II

Feasts of Transition

| Holy Trinity | John 3:16–18 | *God so loved the world* |
| Body and Blood | John 6:51–58 | *This is the bread from heaven* |

Establishing the Kingdom

11 Ordinary Time	Matthew 9:36—10:8	Go after the lost sheep
12 Ordinary Time	Matthew 10:26–33	Nothing is concealed that will not be revealed
13 Ordinary Time	Matthew 10:37–42	Whoever welcomes me welcomes you
14 Ordinary Time	Matthew 11:25–30	The Son wishes to reveal him

The Kingdom of God Is Like . . .

15 Ordinary Time	Matthew 13:1–23	I use parables when I speak to them
16 Ordinary Time	Matthew 13:24–43	I will open my mouth in parables
17 Ordinary Time	Matthew 13:44–52	The reign of God is like a buried treasure

The Signs of the Kingdom

18 Ordinary Time	Matthew 14:13–21	All those present ate their fill
19 Ordinary Time	Matthew 14:22–33	Beyond doubt, you are the Son of God!
20 Ordinary Time	Matthew 15:21–28	Woman, you have great faith!

Recognition of the Kingdom

21 Ordinary Time	Matthew 16:13–20	You are the Messiah, the Son of God!
22 Ordinary Time	Matthew 16:21–27	He must go to Jerusalem to suffer
23 Ordinary Time	Matthew 18:15–20	Where two or three are gathered in my name

The Challenge of the Kingdom: Discipleship

24 Ordinary Time	Matthew 18:21–35	How often must I forgive?
25 Ordinary Time	Matthew 20:1–16	The last shall be first
26 Ordinary Time	Matthew 21:28–32	Tax collectors and prostitutes are entering
27 Ordinary Time	Matthew 21:33–43	The stone rejected by the builders
28 Ordinary Time	Matthew 22:1–14	The invited are many; the elect are few
29 Ordinary Time	Matthew 22:15–21	Jesus recognized their bad faith
30 Ordinary Time	Matthew 22:34–40	An attempt to trip him up
31 Ordinary Time	Matthew 23:1–12	Only one is your teacher, the Messiah

The Fullness of the Kingdom

32 Ordinary Time	Matthew 25:1–13	You know not the day or the hour
33 Ordinary Time	Matthew 25:14–30	The master settled accounts
34 Ordinary Time	Matthew 25:31–46	When the Son of Man comes in glory

Year B, Mark's gospel

Advent – Christmas

The Kingdom of God Is at Hand!

1 Advent	Mark 13:33–37	Be on guard!

Who Is This Man?

2 Advent	Mark 1:1–8	Prepare the way of the Lord
3 Advent	John 1:6–8, 19–28	*Make straight the ways of the Lord*
4 Advent	Luke 1:26–38	*He will be called Son of the Most High*
Christmas Vigil	Matthew 1:1–25	*A family record*
Christmas	Luke 2:1–14	*There were shepherds keeping watch*
Holy Family	Luke 2:22–40	*Destined for the rise and fall of many*
Mother of God	Luke 2:16–21	*Mary treasured these things*
Epiphany	Matthew 2:1–12	*Here is what the prophet has written*
Baptism of the Lord	Mark 1:7–11	This is my Beloved Son

Ordinary Time I

2 Ordinary Time	John 1:35–42	*Behold the Lamb of God*
3 Ordinary Time	Mark 1:14–20	Come, follow me
4 Ordinary Time	Mark 1:21–28	A spirit of authority
5 Ordinary Time	Mark 1:29–39	He would not permit the demons to speak
6 Ordinary Time	Mark 1:40–45	Not a word to anyone
7 Ordinary Time	Mark 2:1–12	We have never seen anything like this
8 Ordinary Time	Mark 2:18–22	No one puts new wine in old wineskins
9 Ordinary Time	Mark 2:23 — 3:6	The Son of Man is lord of the sabbath
10 Ordinary Time	Mark 3:20–35	Who are my mother and my brothers?

Lent

1 Lent	Mark 1:12–15	Put to the test by Satan
2 Lent	Mark 9:2–10	Not to tell anyone
3 Lent	John 2:13–25	*In three days I will raise it up*
4 Lent	John 3:14–21	*Light has come into the world*
5 Lent	John 12:20–33	*Unless a grain of wheat fall into the ground and die*
Passion Sunday	Mark 11:1–10	Blessed is the one who comes
	Mark 14:1—15:47	He was silent and did not answer
Holy Thursday	John 13:1–15	*As I have done, so you must do*
Good Friday	John 18:1—19:42	*King of the Jews*

Easter

Easter Vigil	Mark 16:1–8	They said nothing to anyone
Easter Morning	John 20:1–9	*John saw and believed*
Easter Evening	Luke 24:13–35	*Were not our hearts burning inside us?*
2 Easter	John 20:19–31	*To help you believe that Jesus is the Messiah*
3 Easter	Luke 24:13–35	*Everything written about me must be fulfilled*
4 Easter	John 10:11–18	*I lay down my life*
5 Easter	John 15:1–8	*I am the vine, you are the branches*
6 Easter	John 15:9–17	*The command I give you is this: Love one another*
7 Easter	John 17:11–19	*They do not belong to the world*
Pentecost	John 15:26–27, 16:12–15	*The Spirit will guide you*

Ordinary Time II

Feasts of Transition

| Trinity Sunday | Matthew 28:16–20 | *Make disciples of all the nations* |
| Body and Blood | Mark 14:12–16ff | Take and eat . . . take and drink |

The Secret of the Kingdom

11 Ordinary Time	Mark 4:26–34	The Kingdom of God is like a mustard seed
12 Ordinary Time	Mark 4:35–41	Who can this be?
13 Ordinary Time	Mark 5:21–43	He enjoined them strictly not to tell anyone
14 Ordinary Time	Mark 6:1–6	Where did he get all this?
15 Ordinary Time	Mark 6:7–13	He began to send them out two by two
16 Ordinary Time	Mark 6:30–34	They were like sheep without a shepherd
17 Ordinary Time	John 6:1–15	*The Bread of Life discourse*
18 Ordinary Time	John 6:24–35	*The Bread of Life discourse*
19 Ordinary Time	John 6:41–51	*The Bread of Life discourse*
20 Ordinary Time	John 6:51–58	*The Bread of Life discourse*
21 Ordinary Time	John 6:60–69	*The Bread of Life discourse*

The Secret of True Discipleship

22 Ordinary Time	Mark 7:1–8ff	Why do your disciples not follow the tradition?
23 Ordinary Time	Mark 7:31–37	He enjoined them strictly not to tell anyone
24 Ordinary Time	Mark 8:27–35	You are the messiah!
25 Ordinary Time	Mark 9:30–37	The Son of Man will be delivered up
26 Ordinary Time	Mark 9:38–43ff	Anyone who is not against us is with us
27 Ordinary Time	Mark 10:2–16	To just such as these the Kingdom of God belongs
28 Ordinary Time	Mark 10:17–30	He went away sad, for he had many possessions
29 Ordinary Time	Mark 10:35–45	Not to be served but to serve
30 Ordinary Time	Mark 10:46–52	Immediately he received his sight
31 Ordinary Time	Mark 12:28–34	You are not far from the Reign of God
32 Ordinary Time	Mark 12:38–44	She gave from her want, all that she had

The Kingdom of God Is at Hand!

33 Ordinary Time	Mark 13:24–32	Then you will see the Son of Man
34 Ordinary Time	John 18:33–37	*My kingdom does not belong to this world*

Year C, Luke's gospel

Advent-Christmas

Beginning at the End

1 Advent	**Luke 21:25–28, 34–36**	**You will see the Son of Man!**

Heralding a New Beginning

2 Advent	Luke 3:1–6	All flesh shall see the salvation of God
3 Advent	Luke 3:10–18	Crowds, tax collectors and soldiers
4 Advent	Luke 1:39–45	Blessed is she who trusted the Lord

Tidings of Great Joy for the Whole People

Christmas Vigil	Matthew 1:1–25	*A family record*
Christmas	Luke 2:1–14	There were shepherds keeping watch
Holy Family	Luke 2:41–52	Jesus progessed in grace and maturity
Mother of God	Luke 2:16–21	Mary treasured these things
Epiphany	Matthew 2:1–12	*We observed his star at its rising*
Baptism of the Lord	Luke 3:15–16, 21–22	You are my beloved son

Ordinary Time I

Jesus in Galilee

2 Ordinary Time	John 2:1–12	*A wedding at Cana in Galilee*
3 Ordinary Time	Luke 1:1–4; 4:14–21	Good news to the poor

4 Ordinary Time	Luke 4:21–30	Widows and lepers and Gentiles
5 Ordinary Time	Luke 5:1–11	They left everything and became his followers
6 Ordinary Time	Luke 6:17, 20–26	Blest are you poor; woe to you rich
7 Ordinary Time	Luke 6:27–38	Be as compassionate as your Father is
8 Ordinary Time	Luke 6:39–45	A good tree does not produce bad fruit
9 Ordinary Time	Luke 7:1–10	Not even in Israel have I found such faith
10 Ordinary Time	Luke 7:11–17	A great prophet has risen among us

Lent

Preparing for the Journey

| 1 Lent | Luke 4:1–13 | Jesus was led by the Spirit into the desert |
| 2 Lent | Luke 9:28–36 | Awakening, they saw his glory . . . |

Welcoming Sinners

3 Lent	Luke 13:1–9	Leave it another year; then perhaps it will bear
4 Lent	Luke 15:1–3, 11–32	This man welcomes sinners and eats with them
5 Lent	John 8:1–11	*Let the one without sin cast the first stone*
Passion Sunday	Luke 19:28–40	Blessed is he who comes as king
	Luke 22:14 — 23:56	The crowds returned beating their breasts
Holy Thursday	John 13:1–15	*Lord, are you going to wash my feet?*
Good Friday	John 18:1—19:42	*Blood and water flowed out*

Easter

Everyone Who Believes Has Forgiveness

Easter Vigil	Luke 24:1–12	Why search for the living among the dead?
Easter Morning	John 20:1–9	*John saw and believed*
Easter Evening	Luke 24:13–35	Were not our hearts burning inside us?

From Jerusalem to the Ends of the Earth

Though John's gospel is the source of the gospel readings during Easter, we continue to hear from Luke as author of the Acts of the Apostles. This makes Year C particularly rich; the gospel and Acts are best seen as Luke's two-volume work, the one complementing the other.

2 Easter	Acts 5:12–16	More and more believers were added to the Lord
	John 20:19–31	*At the sight of the Lord, the disciples rejoiced*
3 Easter	Acts 5:27–32, 40–41	Better to obey God than men!
	John 21:1–19	*Simon, son of John, do you love me?*
4 Easter	Acts 13:14, 43–52	The Gentiles responded to the word with praise
	John 10:27–30	*The Father and I are one.*
5 Easter	Acts 14:21–27	He opened the door of faith to the Gentiles
	John 13:31–35	*I give you a new commandment: love*
6 Easter	Acts 15:1–2, 22–29	No burden beyond that which is necessary
	John 14:23–29	*"Peace" is my farewell to you*

7 Easter	Acts 7:55–60	Lord, do not hold this sin against them
	John 17:20–26	*These have known that you sent me*
Pentecost	Acts 2:1–11	Each hears in his own tongue!
	John 20:19–23	*Receive the Holy Spirit*

Ordinary Time II

Feasts of Transition

| Holy Trinity | John 16:12–15 | *The Spirit of truth will guide you to all truth* |
| Body and Blood | Luke 9:11–17 | What they had left...filled twelve baskets |

The Journey to Jerusalem

11 Ordinary Time	Luke 7:36 — 8:3	Your faith has been your salvation
12 Ordinary Time	Luke 9:18–24	Who do you say that I am?
13 Ordinary Time	Luke 9:51–62	Whoever looks back is unfit for the kingdom
14 Ordinary Time	Luke 10:1–12, 17–20	Say to them, "The reign of God is at hand"
15 Ordinary Time	Luke 10:25–37	Which of these was neighbor?

At Prayer

| 16 Ordinary Time | Luke 10:38–42 | Mary has chosen the better portion |
| 17 Ordinary Time | Luke 11:1–13 | Lord, teach us to pray |

The Cost and the Joy of Discipleship

18 Ordinary Time	Luke 12:13–21	Avoid greed in all its forms
19 Ordinary Time	Luke 12:32–48	When much has been given, much is required
20 Ordinary Time	Luke 12:49–53	I have come for division!
21 Ordinary Time	Luke 13:22–30	People from east, west, north, south . . .
22 Ordinary Time	Luke 14:1, 7–14	Invite beggars, the crippled, lame, blind
23 Ordinary Time	Luke 14:25–33	To be disciples you must carry the cross
24 Ordinary Time	Luke 15:1–32	Joy in heaven over one repentant sinner
25 Ordinary Time	Luke 16:1–13	You cannot give yourself to God and money
26 Ordinary Time	Luke 16:19–31	If someone would go to them from the dead
27 Ordinary Time	Luke 17:5–10	Faith the size of a mustard seed
28 Ordinary Time	Luke 17:11–19	This man was a Samaritan

All . . . ALL Are Saved!

29 Ordinary Time	Luke 18:1–8	Will the Son of Man find faith on the earth?
30 Ordinary Time	Luke 18:9–14	Those who humble themselves will be exalted
31 Ordinary Time	Luke 19:1–10	To search out and to save what was lost

Transition to Advent

32 Ordinary Time	Luke 20:27–38	Children of the resurrection, children of God
33 Ordinary Time	Luke 21:5–19	By patient endurance you will save your lives
34 Ordinary Time	Luke 23:35–43	This day you will be with me in paradise!

6 *Preparation for Proclamation*

All that we have discussed so far is preparation for proclamation, but a more remote kind of preparation. Now we turn to the immediate process that readers use to prepare for a specific proclamation event. In what follows, there is no wish to legislate the right (or even the best) way to prepare a given reading. Experienced readers gradually find methods and resources that suit them best. It is important, however, that readers remain open to new methods and new resources so that their ministry continues to grow and deepen.

Prayer and meditation

"May the Lord be in my heart and on my lips that I might worthily proclaim. . . ." It is easy to forget, amidst the work of honing communication skills and studying, that we are in the service of the Lord in proclaiming the word to our fellow Christians. Without maintaining and nourishing our relationship with the Word made flesh, we can hardly expect to be genuine ministers of the words of scripture — where that incarnate Word is revealed.

The study of sacred scripture, whether for personal devotion or in preparation for proclamation, makes prayer an almost spontaneous response. But it is possible for the spontaneity to wane after some time, and our involvement with the word of God can take on the characteristics of a purely scientific research project. There's nothing wrong with bringing the very best of scientific technique to our study — indeed, the better equipped we are for knowing the cultural, linguistic and historical milieu in which the scriptures were written, the better chance we have of discovering the fullest intention of the authors. God inspires human instruments to reveal the divine plan, and they respond, as we have seen, through the filter of their own experience.

The sacred scriptures have proved for many to be the springboard to a new and richer form of prayer. For one who is called to be a minister of the word, this would seem inevitable. The reader who has included prayer in the process of preparing a text is sure to bring the power, conviction and sensitivity of that prayer to the proclamation of it.

Personal study

Abundant study resources are available to readers today and are well within the ability of the average person to understand. The challenge is not in finding the resources but in committing oneself to the time and effort required for intelligent and sensitive proclamation. We can no longer be satisfied with a simple reading of the words — we have all had the experience of hearing a reader trying to deal with a text he or she does not understand. The assembled worshipers cannot be aided in their celebration of faith when this occurs.

Sacred scripture can be read with profit even without studying it. But the scriptures are certainly more complex and far richer than many seem to realize. It has, after all, been the subject of worldwide scholarship and study since it first appeared — and there is no sign of its depths being exhausted. The point is that one who would be a minister of the word must be committed to the kind of long-term, concentrated study that opens the scriptures ever more widely. And the commitment must be motivated by a profound sense of mission and service.

Group study and discussion — working as a team

I received the following letter one day from a longtime user of *Workbook for Lectors and Gospel Readers:*

> Dear Dr. Rosser,
>
> Our Monday evening scripture sharing group at St. Bridget's has been using *Workbook for Lectors and Gospel* Readers for several years, and we have found it to be, in general, very helpful as we try to deepen our understanding and appreciation of the Bible and its relation to the liturgical year.
>
> (signed) Allison Griffin
> *on behalf of St. Bridget's scripture sharing group*

This letter appears here because it is first-hand testimony to the value of a group approach to scripture study guided by resource material.

Many faith communities can testify to the special benefits that come from scripture study groups. Those who exercise the ministry of reader are in a position to reap those benefits in a unique way.

Those who proclaim the word also need ongoing evaluation of their proclamation and communication skills. At the very least, you should allow yourself to be critiqued by a trusted friend or family member who will be honest and objective with you. Even better, those who serve as ministers of the word should gather from time to time and work as a group in providing mutual feedback and encouraging continued growth. A certain breadth of view must characterize such sessions. There is no expectation or wish that all readers sound alike; each person brings a separate and distinct charism to this ministry. On the other hand, the group should establish very clearly and early on that hypersensitivity to criticism must be surrendered. Good service is best evaluated by those who are served, not by the servers.

Consulting the available sources

While the ministry of reader does not require a scholar's understanding of the Bible or biblical criticism, you will certainly want to learn as much as you can about the sacred texts you proclaim. Listed below are some resources that provide good information on the Bible. Many of them should be available at a good bookstore or at your local library.

General works on the Bible

For a general overview on reading the Bible, see:

Raymond E. Brown, *The Critical Meaning of the Bible: How a Modern Reading of the Bible Challenges Christians, the Church, and the Churches.* New York: Paulist Press, 1981.

Etienne Carpentier, *How to Read the Old Testament.* London: SCM Press, 1982.

Etienne Carpentier, *How to Read the New Testament.* London: SCM Press, 1982.

Bible dictionaries

Dictionaries of the Bible are useful when you encounter unfamiliar terms. Comprehensive in their coverage of biblical persons, geography, ancient culture and theological concepts, the two Bible dictionaries listed here differ in the depth of their scholarship.

Harper's Bible Dictionary is a relatively small but comprehensive volume.

The *Anchor Bible Dictionary* is a weighty six-volume work. (This is a resource only if you have quite a lot of time to dedicate to your inquiry!)

Though it is not technically a dictionary, Joseph M. Staudacher's *Lector's Guide to Biblical Pronunciations* (Our Sunday Visitor, 1979) is probably the easiest pronunciation guide available today. Staudacher employs a method for sounding out biblical names and places that will be perhaps much more useful to many than the diacritical markings used in formal dictionaries.

Multi-volume series on the Bible

There are three series on the Bible currently available from The Liturgical Press. They are *The New Testament Message, The Old Testament Message* and *The Message of Biblical Spirituality.* The volumes in these series are both informative and accessible to the nonscholar. Each volume of *The New Testament Message* and *The Old Testament Message* deals with a single book (or group of related books) of the Bible by means of a general introduction followed by commentary on the entire text. *The Message of Biblical Spirituality* draws from the texts to shape a personal or communal spirituality.

Another series of books on the Bible, the *Proclamation Series,* is published by Augsburg Fortress Press. It too deals with the various books of both Testaments, introducing the reader to the theology and history of the authors and the time periods.

Bible commentaries

There are many fine commentaries on Bible texts. Here we recommend a few of the best. The *Collegeville Bible Commentary* from The Liturgical Press provides a usable and accessible explanation of scripture texts.

The New Jerome Biblical Commentary (Prentice Hall, 1990) is written especially for Roman Catholics. In addition to commentaries on the individual books of the Bible, *The New Jerome Biblical Commentary* features informative essays from the Catholic point of view on topics such as inspiration, canonicity, hermeneutics, church pronouncements and the use of the Bible in the early church.

The Women's Bible Commentary (John Knox Press, 1992) deals with biblical texts relevant to women's issues.

Paulist Press publishes the *What Are They Saying?* series, which covers many topics of interest to Roman Catholics; many of these topics deal with the history and theology of the Bible.

On the ministry of reading in a public setting

Three works on reading in public that would be beneficial to those who read the scriptures in church are:

Charlotte I. Lee and Frank Galati, *Oral Interpretation*, 7th ed. Boston: Houghton Mifflin Company, 1986.

Michael and Susan Osborn, *Public Speaking*, 2d ed. Boston: Houghton Mifflin Company, 1991.

Joseph M. Staudacher, *Lector's Guide to Biblical Pronunciations*. Huntington, IN: Our Sunday Visitor, 1979.

Understanding the lectionary

Because the lectionary is the liturgical reader's specialty, an understanding of its structure and purpose must be presumed. There is no better brief introduction to the lectionary than Gerard Sloyan's "Overview of the lectionary for Mass," in *The Liturgy Documents: A Parish Resource*, Chicago: Liturgy Training Publications, 1991.

A sample preparation course

As readers gain experience in their ministry and incorporate it into their lives, they discover the methods of preparation that best suit them. Nevertheless, it may be helpful to provide a demonstration of one way to go about preparing for actual proclamation. What follows is only a suggestion.

Begin with prayer. It need not be lengthy, but because you are entering the realm of the inspired word of God, a brief prayer of praise and thanksgiving will enable you to begin your task in a spirit of openness, humility and gratitude. Scripture itself provides the best prayer. Consider, for example, these verses from Psalm 119:

10 With my whole heart I seek you; do not let me stray from your commandments.
11 I treasure your word in my heart, so that I may not sin against you.
12 Blessed are you, O LORD; teach me your statutes.
13 With my lips I declare all the ordinances of your mouth.
14 I delight in the way of your decrees as much as in all riches.
15 I will meditate on your precepts, and fix my eyes on your ways.
16 I will delight in your statutes; I will not forget your word.
17 Deal bountifully with your servant, so that I may live and observe your word.
18 Open my eyes, so that I may behold wondrous things out of your law.

The next step is to open the lectionary and read through all the texts (including the responsorial psalm and the gospel acclamation) assigned for the day on which you are to proclaim. It is important that you gain an overall sense of the dominant themes of a given Sunday. The reading you will proclaim is not isolated but is part of the texture of the whole celebration. Here, for example, are the lectionary texts for the First Sunday of Advent (Year A):

First Reading: *Isaiah 2:1 – 5*

The word that Isaiah son of Amoz saw
concerning Judah and Jerusalem.

In days to come
the mountain of the Lord's house
shall be established as the highest of the mountains,
and shall be raised above the hills;
all the nations shall stream to it.

Many peoples shall come and say,
"Come, let us go up to the mountain of the LORD,
to the house of the God of Jacob;
that he may teach us his ways
and that we may walk in his paths."

For out of Zion shall go forth instruction,
and the word of the LORD from Jerusalem.
He shall judge between the nations,
and shall arbitrate for many peoples;
they shall beat their swords into plowshares,
and their spears into pruning hooks;
nation shall not lift up sword against nation,
neither shall they learn war any more.

O house of Jacob, come,
let us walk in the light of the LORD!

Responsorial Psalm: *Psalm 122:1 – 2, 4 – 9*

I was glad when they said to me,
"Let us go to the house of the LORD!"
Our feet are standing
within your gates, O Jerusalem.

To it the tribes go up, the tribes of the LORD,
as was decreed for Israel,

to give thanks to the name of the LORD.
For there the thrones for judgment were set up,
the thrones of the house of David.

Pray for the peace of Jerusalem:
"May they prosper who love you.
Peace be within your walls,
and security within your towers."

For the sake of my relatives and friends
I will say, "Peace be within you."
For the sake of the house of the LORD our God,
I will seek your good.

Second Reading: *Romans 13:11 – 14*

Brothers and sisters,
You know what time it is,
how it is now the moment for you to wake from sleep.
For salvation is nearer to us now
than when we became believers;
the night is far gone, the day is near.
Let us then lay aside the works of darkness
and put on the armor of light;
let us live honorably as in the day,
not in reveling and drunkenness,
not in debauchery and licentiousness,
not in quarreling and jealousy.

Instead, put on the Lord Jesus Christ,
and make no provision for the flesh, to gratify its desires.

Gospel Acclamation: *Psalm 85:7*

Alleluia.
Lord, show us your mercy and love,
    and grant us your salvation.
Alleluia.

Gospel Reading: *Matthew 24:37 – 44*

Jesus spoke to his disciples:

"As the days of Noah were,
so will be the coming of the Son of Man.

For as in those days before the flood
they were eating and drinking,
marrying and giving in marriage,
until the day Noah entered the ark,
and they knew nothing
until the flood came and swept them all away,
so too will be the coming of the Son of Man.
Then two will be in the field;
one will be taken and one will be left.
Two women will be grinding meal together;
one will be taken and one will be left.

Keep awake, therefore,
for you do not know on what day your Lord is coming.
But understand this:
if the owner of the house had known
in what part of the night the thief was coming,
he would have stayed awake
and would not have let his house be broken into.
Therefore you also must be ready,
for the Son of Man is coming at an unexpected hour."

It is not difficult to see how closely these readings are related. The season of Advent dictates the choice of texts and their central concerns: promise of the coming kingdom of peace, joy in the fulfillment of the Lord's promises, optimism and the need to be prepared. The unity of theme and purpose among all the texts makes each one the richer.

If you have a study resource available, turn to it now. For our present purposes, we have taken the commentaries from *Workbook for Lectors and Gospel Readers* (Year A, 1996). They are brief, non-academic examinations of the readings and have a twofold purpose: first, to extract the intellectual, emotional and aesthetic content of the text, and second, to suggest how the reader might effectively communicate that content, taking into account the liturgical situation, the season, and so forth. A similar two-fold purpose should guide your study and preparation regardless of the resource material you employ.

Commentary on Reading I: Isaiah 2:1 – 5

A new liturgical season begins today. This does not come as a surprise, however, because the readings for the last few Sundays have already introduced the central idea: the completion of God's plan to bring all creation to perfection and unity in divine love.

The season of Advent proclaims that it is with the birth of Jesus that the Kingdom of God on earth becomes present most vividly.

But the great plan of God to restore the world in perfect love began long before the birth of Jesus, and the prophets of Israel saw visions of this restoration many centuries earlier. The prophet Isaiah is a case in point. It is clear that the world he describes in this first reading will be different from the present (his and ours). The difference will be that all people will recognize God's law of love as the only way to universal peace.

You want to hasten these "days to come" as you read the first scripture passage of this new year of grace. Optimism and joy are always a part of beginnings, and your voice can communicate encouragement and hope to the assembly.

The most compelling image here is the picture of nations reshaping their weapons of destruction into farm implements — tools for planting, growing and harvesting. Read this classic image in such a way that the assembly will hear it fresh — perhaps for the first time!

Special notes:

1. *Amos is pronounced AY-muhz.*
2. *The people respond to the vision ("Come, let us go up to the mountain . . ."). A pause and renewed vocal energy are effective. The literary technique Isaiah uses in this poem (and remember as you read it that it is a poem) is parallelism. Almost every line has its parallel in the line which follows. (Example: For out of Zion shall go forth instruction, and the word of the LORD from Jerusalem.) Let the second line in each case be an echo of the first.*
3. *After the people speak, we return to the narrative of the vision.*
4. *The plea "Come . . ." is fervent, an invitation to renewal during the Advent season, when we prepare for the coming of the Lord in new ways.*

Commentary on the Second Reading: Romans 13:11 – 14

Night and day. Darkness and light. Evil and good. Paul tells us in these images that dawn is approaching (the "light of the Lord" in the first reading). Thus the time associated with the darkness of sin must give way to the time associated with the brightness of love. The urgency of Paul's words fit the urgency of Advent. The word is out: God is moving toward us; we've got to move toward God. And that, of course, means moving away from less noble things.

Using images of night and day, Paul even reminds us of the way we dress. Nightgowns and pajamas are not sturdy enough for the work we do during the day; we have to put on warmer and more protective clothing: "the armor of light" and "the Lord Jesus Christ." Once we are clothed in the Lord Jesus, we are equipped for good works.

Special notes:

1. *These are words of comfort and encouragement. Be sure they don't sound like a reprimand or threat.*
2. *Sentences that begin "Let us . . ." are most effective when spoken with great energy and conviction.*
3. *After a series of "nots," the reading ends with a strong contrast.*

Commentary on the gospel reading: Matthew 24:37 – 44

The word "Advent" means "coming" or "arrival." We hear this idea in all three readings today: "In days to come," "the day draws near," and "the coming of the Son of man." We see again that Advent looks back in order to look forward. Jesus does precisely this in reminding us of the time of Noah and the flood. And the purpose for looking back is that we may see ahead more clearly.

In a private session with his chosen twelve, Jesus explains at length what the end of time will be like. Today's reading is only a brief section of Jesus' discourse, and the emphasis is on readiness, on being prepared. It is very easy to get caught up in the flow of day-to-day activities and to become forgetful of the truly important things in life. It happened in Noah's time and it happens in ours. Jesus is not counseling us to live in fear and dread; rather, people are to live in expectation and hope, alert to the signs of God's loving plan to draw the world together.

You cannot avoid a sense of warning as you read this passage to the assembly, but the emphasis is quite positive: We can profit from the lessons of the past; we know what it means to stay awake and not get caught off guard. It means being ready for the many ways that God's love enters our lives.

Special notes:

1. *Jesus, like a good teacher, explains with the use of historical example (Noah).*
2. *The example is applied ("So will it be . . .").*
3. *The final sentence is not so much a warning as a statement of fact.*

No single method of preparation will be effective for everyone, and what each individual reader brings to his or her study will make it unique. And that's how it should be. No single mode of proclamation is prescribed for readers.

7 Liturgical Environment, Vesture, Movement and Decorum

The liturgy may be compared to a symphony, a baseball game or any gathering in which success depends on quality teamwork. Readers are part of the liturgy team, playing their role in full awareness that they are working in concert with many others to create a celebration of faith and worship that will build up the assembled community in faith. Readers who see their task as beginning with "A reading from . . ." and ending with "The word of the Lord" have a mistaken notion of liturgical ministry.

That notion is exemplified in the practice of having the reader emerge from the assembly to proclaim the reading and then immediately rejoin the congregation. The reasons offered for this practice are noble: the reader can worship with his or her family; there is more of an impression of participation by the assembly when the reader is seen more clearly as part of the assembly; a wider notion of "ministry by all the faithful" is expressed. Nevertheless, the church continues to assert that roles of leadership in liturgical worship should be visible from start to finish. It should be apparent that the presider is surrounded by representatives of the assembly for the entire liturgy. The practice of having ministers "pop in" for a given function and then disappear is discouraged.

The church's assertion in this regard is supported by broader views of what liturgy is and how it works. Above all, liturgy is one integral action, not a string of isolated elements. Even the separation into liturgy of the word and liturgy of the eucharist is, ultimately, academic. Those who are called to leadership roles in liturgical worship should reflect the unity and integrity of the worship event by their presence from beginning to end.

In the discussion that follows, there is no wish to contradict or criticize long-established local practice that is in accord with liturgical principles and directives. On the other hand, it is apparent that excessive enthusiasm has, in some communities, introduced practices into the liturgy that can only be called theatrical. Theatre is a noble and powerful art form. There is no intention here to discredit it. But liturgy is not theatre, even when its fullest expression is quite dramatic. The purposes of the two are profoundly different: theatre's purpose is to create a vicarious experience for an audience; liturgy's purpose is to express and celebrate the immediate faith experience of all present.

Posture and attitude (nonverbal language)

Members of the assembly know well that their experience of liturgical worship is affected by the manner in which the leaders of the liturgy conduct themselves. Excessive formality bordering on coldness or arrogance should be just as foreign to our expression of faith as its equally inappropriate opposite: excessive cordiality bordering on false intimacy or sentimentality. Persons of good will and average sensitivity will know almost intuitively that the liturgy requires dignity and restraint, an alert reverence that communicates awareness of the significance of ritual worship. Individual readers may need to be reminded (or shown how) to present themselves, body and spirit, in such a way that the assembly they serve will be edified, not distracted.

Good, relaxed posture, neither stiff nor careless, is a must, not only because of the signal it gives but because it is required for effective use of the body in public communication. Experts in the field remind us over and over that "nonverbal language speaks loudest." Nonverbal language is everything but the words coming from your mouth (including "ahs," "uhs," body language, dress, posture, attitude, and so on). If the way we present ourselves to an audience is disagreeable or distracting, it will drown out anything we have to say. Readers who shift rhythmically from one foot to the other, lean into the microphone or wear enormous dangling earrings allow unfair competition to accompany them to the lectern. Their non-verbal language will drown out their proclamation.

The words "dignity" and "restraint" may carry negative connotations for some readers, but they probably best describe the kind of decorum appropriate for ritual worship. "Mastery of the situation and task" is a phrase that should carry only positive connotations and describes the goal readers should strive for most earnestly. Readers who "master" the functions of their ministry are accorded the kind of credibility that enables them to minister most effectively.

Procession and recessional

In processions and recessionals the reader carries the lectionary (or the gospel book) and follows the servers and cross bearer. The manner of carrying the book varies widely. Holding the book aloft, like a standard or imperial insignia, is excessive no matter how well-intentioned. We show reverence toward many articles in the liturgy — and the book of readings is one of them — but people are more important than things, and it is the reader's presence in the procession that is the point. It is better to carry the book with both hands a few inches in front of the breast. This more modest stance communicates an awareness of being part of a group of ministers, not singled out by exaggerated gesture.

Liturgical books

There are two books used for readings: the lectionary and the book of gospels. Some parishes use only the lectionary, some use both. Because they contain the word of God, they are treated with reverence and respect and are often elaborately decorated with artistically wrought covers. Because they are designed for use at the liturgy, readers should use them — not a missalette or a hymnal containing the readings or even a personally prepared copy of the text. This practice is not uncommon and is even understandable when the reader has marked a more disposable copy of the text in various ways to facilitate better proclamation. Nevertheless, the nobility of the task and the spirit of the liturgy call for the use of a more fitting volume, one that signals the significance of its contents by its very appearance. Perhaps we have here an exception to the rule that you can't tell a book by its cover!

The current rubrics indicate that the reader may carry the gospel book in procession (if there is no deacon) and place it on the altar at the end of the entrance procession. Oddly, this practice has the minister of the word carrying a book from which he or she will not read, since the gospel proclamation is done by the deacon or priest. Though the inconsistency may seem minor, it might be better for the reader to carry the lectionary and for the gospel book, if used, to be placed on the altar ahead of time, as the rubrics also indicate. (In no case should there be two books carried in procession — the gospel book by the deacon *and* the lectionary by the reader.) The reader may then place the lectionary on the lectern at the end of the procession or keep it until it is used for the first reading. In the latter case, a small table should be provided at the reader's chair. Very often one witnesses the lectionary being carried in procession and then placed on the floor next to the reader's chair until it is needed — a practice that sends very mixed signals indeed!

Vesture

What should ministers of the word wear when they perform their ministry? In the case of the gospel reader (a deacon or priest), the question is answered in the rubrics. For readers who are laypersons, the question is open and has provoked some rather strong feelings and opinions. Practices vary from place to place. Some insist that lay readers should wear no special clothing and therefore appear more representative of the assembly from which they have been called for this ministry. Lay readers in lay dress would seem, in this view, to signal greater lay participation in the liturgy. A different view sees value in according the ministry of reader (and therefore the word itself) greater prominence by distinctive dress, such as an alb (the basic liturgical garment).

The following considerations may be helpful to individuals, liturgy teams and entire faith communities in deciding how to approach the matter of vesture for readers other than priests and deacons. One view of the ministry of reader would see the one who proclaims the word as a lay person called to perform a specific task at the liturgy; another, and broader view would see the reader as someone chosen for formation into ministry and commissioned to perform that ministry within the faith community. The difference is that the first view emphasizes a limited function, whereas the second emphasizes the reader's role in the community.

The church's tradition would seem to support the second view. Until very recently, the ministry of reader was one of the "minor orders" (acolyte, porter, reader, exorcist). In modern times the minor orders were, in effect, steps toward priesthood, culminating in the "major orders" (subdeacon, deacon and priest). But the point is that the candidate was "ordained" to the office of reader, which implies something more than occasional function — it implies formation into the office and a certain authority to exercise it.

When the ministry of reader is seen as something far greater than an occasional task performed in the liturgy, greater emphasis and significance are placed on the proclamation of the word of God. Our question then becomes: Can vesture signal emphasis on the importance of the reader's function and role in proclaiming the word? If so, then its use is not only justified but recommended. Those who feel that no exterior sign is necessary for such emphasis to be given to the word in proclamation will have to explain the abundance of such signs in all ritual activity.

Finally, and very practically, liturgical vesture for the reader (the alb) not only emphasizes the role of the wearer but also solves the issue of appropriate dress for liturgical ministry. Recommendations about "nothing too flashy, nothing to distract the hearers" and the difficulties involved in defining such terms become irrelevant.

Lectern and microphone

Readers have very practical concerns regarding the stand that holds the lectionary and the equipment necessary for amplifying the human voice in large worship spaces. The ideal lectern is of simple design — strong enough to hold the book but not so bulky as to hide the reader. Further, if the lectern height is adjustable and the surface that holds the book can be tilted at varying degrees, readers of various sizes can be better accommodated. Some older churches have enormous elevated pulpits that are now used for all the readings. Persons of small stature are sometimes barely visible. This situation should be remedied by having a more suitable lectern built or purchased. At the very least, readers need to assess the situation beforehand and be creative in solving problems of height and angle.

The microphone at the lectern is, potentially, even more problematic. Modern technology and the science of acoustics have made it possible to solve the sound problems of even the most cavernous buildings. All is for naught, however, if the reader does not know how to use the microphone correctly. And even in the best of circumstances, readers are sometimes at the mercy of the vagaries of sophisticated equipment. The only useful rule of thumb is twofold: First, experiment at length, with the help of others, to find out how you and your voice are best served by your situation; second, avoid the common mistake of believing that the amplification system will do most of the work for you. The microphone is simply an aid — nothing more. It will not make a poor reading good — only louder! You should be able to ignore it completely once it is turned on. Do not lean into it; do not back off from it. Most microphones should never be more than twelve inches from your mouth; some should be considerably less than that. Finally, you must lift and project your voice (see the section on pitch and volume) according to the size of the space regardless of the amplification system.

8 *Special Modes of Proclamation*

The ordinary mode of proclamation is what we see most of the time: One reader at the lectern proclaims the assigned reading. But there are times when alternate modes of proclamation will enhance worship by adding interest, clarity and immediacy to longer readings, special readings and even special gatherings that celebrate the word outside of the liturgical context. There is no intention here to recommend "gimmicks" in the hope of forestalling boredom. The guiding principle is the same as it is everywhere in this book: to enhance the assembly's experience of the word of God so that it may be fulfilled in their hearing.

Multiple readers

Multiple readers, assigned various parts of a given text, are nothing new in the church's liturgy. For centuries, the accounts of the Lord's Passion on Palm Sunday and Good Friday were proclaimed (sung, and in Latin) by three readers: the *Evangelistus,* who read the words of the gospel writer; the *Synagogus,* who took the words of "the crowd" and persons other than Jesus; and the *Christus,* who read the words of Jesus himself. The chant settings further distinguished the three by composing them in three ranges (middle for the narrator, high for persons other than Jesus, and low for the *Christus*). Sung by three accomplished cantors, the Passion was unforgettable when presented in this way.

When the objective is to place emphasis on a particularly important text or to celebrate an unusually significant liturgical event within a given community, there is no reason why other readings throughout the liturgical year cannot employ multiple readers. In fact, our experience of special seasons and feasts can be greatly enhanced by placing particular emphasis on the scripture readings. A primary consideration is the amount of time and energy required to ensure that multiple readers will do a creditable job; it takes quite a lot of practice to render this mode of proclamation truly listenable!

The Passion

The Passion is still proclaimed in the way described above, except that in most communities in America it is read rather than sung, and is, of course, almost always in English. There are several ways in which the text may be divided among readers. For those who are not familiar with this practice, here is a sample from one arrangement of the Passion according to John:

First reader:
So Jesus came out, wearing the crown of thorns and the purple robe. Pilate said to them,

Second reader:
"Here is the man!"

First reader:
When the chief priests and the police saw him, they shouted,

Congregation:
"Crucify him! Crucify him!"

First reader:
Pilate said to them,

Second reader:
"Take him yourselves and crucify him; I find no case against him."

First reader:
The Jews answered him,

Congregation:
"We have a law, and according to that law he ought to die because he has claimed to be the Son of God."

First reader:
Now when Pilate heard this, he was more afraid than ever. He entered his headquarters again and asked Jesus,

Second reader:
"Where are you from?"

First reader:
But Jesus gave him no answer. Pilate therefore said to him,

Second reader:
"Do you refuse to speak to me? Do you not know that I have power to release you, and power to crucify you?"

First reader:
Jesus answered him,

Third reader:
"You would have no power over me unless it had been given you from above; therefore the one who handed me over to you is guilty of a greater sin."

In this example, the text has been divided among three readers and the entire congregation. Other arrangements have the congregation speak all the words except those of the evangelist and Jesus. Still other arrangements omit connecting words that introduce speech, such as "Jesus answered him" and "Pilate said to them." At some point, this mode of presentation may begin to resemble re-enactment rather than proclamation. When the readers begin to take on the "character" of the person or persons whose words they are reading, we approach a mode of presentation more suitable for theatre or dramatic interpretation than for liturgy.

The practice of having the entire assembly take the part of "the crowd" may deserve reconsideration. The intent, of course, is to achieve greater participation on the part of all the worshipers, or perhaps it is to enable them to feel more "involved" in the proclamation. The effect, however, is that when all are proclaimers, none are hearers. Perhaps we underestimate the sacramentality of receiving the word through listening, through being "hearers" of the word. A purely practical consideration, with sacramental consequences, is that "the crowd" must follow along in their copies of the text if they are to perform their part. Thus, their role as hearers is reduced even further. It may be worth our while to reconsider this practice.

The Sundays of Lent

On the third, fourth and fifth Sundays of Lent, the readings from Year A may be proclaimed during Years B and C. The reason is that these texts are particularly important for the instruction of catechumens, which ideally takes place during the Lenten season. The gospel texts for the three Sundays are: Jesus' encounter with the Samaritan woman (Third Sunday of Lent, John 4:4 – 42), the story of the man born blind (Fourth Sunday of Lent, John 9:1 – 41) and the story of the raising of Lazarus from the dead (Fifth Sunday of Lent, John 11:1 – 45). Because these gospel texts are longer than usual, significant for their instructional value for catechumens and include a lot of dialogue, they may be particularly suited for proclamation by multiple readers.

The second readings for these three Sundays in Lent could also be proclaimed by multiple readers, most effectively, perhaps, by two. They are all discourses from Paul's letters to the Romans (third and fifth Sundays) and to the Ephesians (fourth Sunday) and are particularly rich in fundamental statements about Christian discipleship. Here, for example, is an arrangement for two readers of the second reading for the Fourth Sunday of Lent (Year A). The central metaphor is light and darkness, and is closely associated with the gospel story of the man born blind.

Ephesians 5:8 – 14

First reader:
A reading from the letter of Paul to the Ephesians

Second reader:
Once you were darkness, but now in the Lord you are light.
Live as children of light —

First reader:
for the fruit of the light is found in all that is good and right and true.

Second reader:
Try to find out what is pleasing to the Lord.

First reader:
Take no part in the unfruitful works of darkness,
but instead expose them.

Second reader:
For it is shameful even to mention
what such people do secretly;

First reader:
but everything exposed by the light becomes visible,

Second reader:
for everything that becomes visible is light.
Therefore it says,

BOTH READERS:
"Sleeper, awake! Rise from the dead,
and Christ will shine on you."

First reader:
The Word of the Lord.

It is important to remember that whenever multiple readers are employed in the context of the liturgy, they are still readers — ministers of the word, not actors who impersonate characters or strive for a re-enactment of the text. They still relate to the hearers through the medium of the printed word — they still *read*.

Because special arrangements of the text will require multiple copies, these should be placed in handsome binders worthy of the liturgical environment. There should be no impression that the readers have memorized the text or that this is their own rendition of the reading. It must be very clear to the assembly that they are hearing the word of God in sacred scripture proclaimed to them as usual — except that a different mode of proclamation is being employed for a very good and carefully explicated reason.

Memorized presentations of the word

Though there are some who believe that memorized presentations — complete with gestures, staged movements and characterizations — are potentially the most effective way to proclaim the word, I must disagree. The role of the reader is to read. The medium is the word of God as recorded in sacred scripture, and it is important that the book be involved in liturgical proclamation. A memorized presentation will always put the reader rather than the text into the foreground, emphasizing the performance above the content. Outside the context of the liturgy such presentations are potentially inspiring, informative and entertaining. But within the liturgy itself, they fall outside the purpose of ritual worship, which is to celebrate the faith held in common by the gathered community. The word of God as recorded in the Bible is *proclaimed* at the liturgy. It is *not* re-enacted or performed. It would be better to leave memorized presentations to celebrations of the word outside the context of liturgy, as discussed below.

Other celebrations of the word

The texts of the Bible have been presented in many effective ways outside the context of the liturgy. For a time immediately following the Second Vatican Council, a form of worship called the "Bible vigil" was quite popular. Essentially a series of readings and meditations on the word of God, these worship services introduced the faithful — in new and exciting ways — to sacred scripture as a springboard to prayer.

Because they are celebrated apart from the official liturgy of the church, such services can take on whatever character and arrangement seems appropriate to the situation or event they commemorate, or to the community in which they take place. Very often they are ecumenical services that bring Christians from various denominations together in prayer and celebration of the word of God.

Interpretive or dramatic readings, staged readings

Certain sections of the Bible lend themselves particularly well to dramatization. This is evidenced by a long and uninterrupted history of biblical plays, films and television dramas. The parables of the gospels seem especially well suited for such adaptation because they are, in effect, dramas complete with plot, characters, conflict and resolution. Ministers of the word are in a position to assume leadership and direction in such efforts.

If your community is also blessed with someone who is a talented dramatist, you may be able to offer a program of scripture study that will be greatly enhanced by well-executed stagings of biblical literature. A well-organized and ambitious group of readers could witness a resurgence of interest in sacred scripture in their community in response to a Friday evening Lenten program at which the gospel stories of the following Sunday were dramatized. Such a program also would include discussions of the other readings and, of course, prayer.

9 *Texts Other than the Assigned Readings*

The reader is sometimes called upon to present or proclaim texts other than the assigned readings. Though a less than ideal liturgical practice, it is allowed for in the liturgical directives and is sometimes unavoidable in smaller faith communities. When the reader is recruited for such functions, all the principles of effective communication and liturgical proclamation are applicable.

Introductions, commentaries and announcements

Introductions to the readings should always be brief and are usually unnecessary. The same is true for commentary on the liturgical rites. The role of the commentator was more significant during the liturgical renewal following Vatican II, when many changes required explanation even during the liturgy. The practice has declined sharply now that the new rites are familiar, and it is useful only when special liturgies (such as the ordination of priests or bishops, or the rite of monastic profession) are celebrated. Commentary can also be beneficial at liturgies such as marriages and funerals if those liturgies are attended by significant numbers of people of other faiths or denominations. Simplicity must be the guiding principle when constructing commentary, and the reading of it should be carefully planned so that it truly assists the assembly and does not interrupt the prayerful flow of the celebration.

Announcements about matters concerning the assembled community (such as the time of the next parish council meeting) should be printed in a bulletin. When it is necessary to make such announcements during the liturgy, the proper time is immediately after the closing prayer and before the blessing. Clearly, a more informal tone will characterize the reading of such texts.

Responsorial psalm

The responsorial psalm follows the first reading and an intervening pause for reflection. The responsorial psalm is by definition a sung response, but it may be recited if singing it is not possible. The reader is very often expected to lead the assembly when this is the case. Because it calls for a refrain by the assembly interspersed with verses by the reader, the assembly must hear clear vocal cues in the reader's voice so that they know when to repeat the refrain. Usually a downward pitch in the voice signals the assembly's response. It may take some practice to learn how to make this signal clear.

The gospel acclamation (Alleluia and verse) is meant to be sung by the cantor and assembly. If it is not sung, it is to be omitted. It should never be read. To recite it in a speaking tone sounds a trifle ridiculous.

General intercessions

The general intercessions, or prayers of the faithful, are sometimes announced by the reader. Whether or not you, as reader, compose the intercessions, remember that they are invitations to prayer, not prayers themselves. It is very common to hear the general intercessions phrased like this: "Lord, we ask you to watch over the entire church, the pope and bishops, and all your faithful people; for this we pray to the Lord." Clearly, this is not an invitation to prayer but a prayer itself. As an invitation, the text would read like this: "Let us ask the Lord to watch over the entire church . . . ; we pray to the Lord." You will probably want to vary the phrasing to avoid a stereotypical drone. (It takes only about three "Let us's" in a row before people begin having images of a green salad!) Some examples: "We pray for the church . . ." "The church is the Body of Christ. We pray for . . ." or simply, "For the church on earth, that . . ."

Unlike the responsorial psalm, the general intercessions include a formula that concludes each invitation and signals the assembly's response. The intercessions invite the assembly to unite in prayer (with a well-known formula such as "Lord, hear our prayer") for a stated purpose, concern or person. The sequence of intentions usually follows this pattern:

(a) for the needs of the church,

(b) for public authorities and the salvation of the world,

(c) for those oppressed by any need,

(d) for the local community

(e) for special needs/occasions (at weddings, funerals, etc.)

Postcommunion meditation

After the communion rite has ended, there should be a period of silence, a hymn of praise sung by the assembly or a psalm sung or recited. If the text is spoken, it may be done by the reader. If this task falls to you as reader, your intention must be to create a spirit of thankful and joyful prayer. It is a meditative moment, so the manner of your presentation will be different from that employed for the proclamation of a reading. Nevertheless, of course, you must be heard.

10 Establishing and Sustaining the Ministry of Reader

I remember quite vividly a question put to me by a pastor in Kansas City, Missouri, several years ago: "Should I just put out a general call for lectors and take whatever comes forward?" My response was something like this: "Oh, my, no! First you want to publish a little something in your bulletin about the ministry of reader, the basic skills required, and, above all, the significance of this ministry. Then you probably want to have something like 'auditions,' though you don't want to call them that."

The final section of this book provides suggestions for initiating a carefully planned reader formation program in the parish community. It seems there are plenty of people who are willing to take on such a task and who realize the potential benefit of such a program, but they are not sure how to begin. What follows arises from my years of experience with working with parish programs for readers — some of which are very successful. Other communities have tried and failed to keep a reader formation program alive and well. There is no attempt here to formulate an approach guaranteed to work in every community; there are only suggestions that may be welcome and some observations about what has worked and what has not.

Assessing the current situation

First we must deal with a very common situation: "occasional" or "guest" readers. These are the sisters, cousins and aunts who are asked to "do the reading" at a relative's wedding or funeral or on some other special occasion. This practice stems from the innocent notion that anyone who can read can proclaim the scriptures. This entire book is dedicated to the conviction that such is not the case. Effective proclamation can be done only by those who have been called and formed into the ministry of reader.

After all, Uncle Bob is not a priest and so is not asked to officiate. If Aunt Mildred is not a singer, she is not asked to be the cantor. If Sister Cecily is not an organist, she is not asked to be a minister of music. If nephews Billy and Chuck are not altar servers, they will at least have to be taught how to function in that role. At the very least, if only because it seems likely that the practice will not disappear overnight, "guest" readers should be required to prepare for this one-time exercise of the ministry with an experienced reader who can give instruction and guidance.

In many communities it will fall to the pastor or to a pastoral associate to inaugurate a reader formation program or improve upon one already in place. But there is no reason why such initiative cannot be exercised by someone else. The most effective initiative seems to emerge from readers themselves who feel the need for deeper and more sustained formation.

It is important to assess your current situation before launching a formation program or attempting to enhance the program already in place. Most parishes already have a group of generous laypersons who serve as readers at the liturgy. And, of course, priests and deacons who proclaim the gospel are ministers of the word and must also be included in all deliberations. An initial step would be to canvass all those who serve as readers and get a clear picture of the status of the ministry in your community as perceived by those who exercise it. "How are we doing?" is the governing question. Written forms or questionnaires may be used at first, but at some point very early on in the process round-table discussions should be held.

Small parishes may be able to conduct a discussion with all the readers together. Larger communities that have, say, more than a dozen readers should break into smaller groups, direct the discussion through the use of a prepared set of questions (or a tabulation of questionnaire results) and then hear reports from each group on the results of their discussion. Although you may feel that a wider assessment of the ministry would be helpful — from the liturgy team, the parish council, even the entire parish community — experience has shown that such broad canvassing gets a poor response and is frequently interpreted as negative criticism of the status quo. On the other hand, it is probably a very good idea to announce in the bulletin that your readers are meeting to discuss their ministry and that interested parties are invited to attend.

The purpose of this initial step is not to invite criticism and is certainly not to provide an opportunity for personal critiques of individual readers. Rather, it is to get a sense of your readers' experience of their proclamation of the word and to obtain their suggestions for making it more efficacious — for themselves and the assembly. The sustained presumption must be that the ministers of the word are eager to enhance their skills and serve the community more effectively. Thus, the statements and questions guiding the discussions must be entirely positive.

The results of such discussions, judging from my experience with them, will probably fall into two categories: immediate problems and difficulties, and more substantive comments relevant to formation and growth. In the first category, expect comments like these: "I'm not sure they're listening." "Can I be heard?" "Can we do something about crying babies and other noise?" "Why do the ushers keep seating latecomers during the readings?" "I don't think our public address system is adequate." "The lectern is too high (or low)." "I need more advance notice; don't call me at 10:00 AM and ask me to read at the 11:00 o'clock mass." "I can never find the right place in the lectionary."

Though these observations may seem not all that important, even picayune, when compared to such matters as "scripture study," they are an opportunity to establish credibility in the seriousness of plans for a thorough formation program — if they are carefully examined and acted upon immediately. Have the public address system checked out. Instruct the ushers to hold latecomers back until the reading is finished. Fix the lectern. Improve the system by which readers are assigned and give them adequate notice. Give instruction on how the lectionary is arranged. Provide every reader with an inexpensive paperback copy of the lectionary. Nothing will dispose readers more favorably toward their ministry than prompt attention to the problems they face — problems rather easily solved.

The second category of comments is, in effect, a request for substantive formation. "Sometimes I don't understand what I'm reading; how can I hope to communicate it?" "We need a good set of scripture commentaries made available." "Aren't there books on the market specifically to help readers do their job?" "I get so nervous!" "We need more people to share this ministry." "I'm not sure I'm getting it across; I need feedback." "I get called upon too often (too seldom)." "Maybe we should have a workshop or call in an expert." It is in responding to these kinds of observations and concerns that the need for an ongoing formation program becomes apparent to all.

Sending out the call

Once there is a general sense of the group's concerns and needs, the call goes out. But the call is not simply an invitation to participate in the ministry. It is addressed to the entire parish community and appears first as a series of inserts in the bulletin or as a series of homilies (on days when the readings render it appropriate) on "Proclamation of the Word of God." Several readings during the season of Advent provide the perfect opportunity for centering the celebration's emphasis on the word of God and the means by which it continues to be proclaimed in our day. *The Constitution on the Sacred Liturgy* of Vatican II has striking things to say about sacred scripture, the ministry of the reader and liturgical proclamation ("It is Christ himself who speaks"). Liturgical reform has resulted in the church's view of itself as a "people of the book" as well as a "people of the table."

It is a serious mistake to view a reader formation program as an effort involving only those who exercise that ministry. In effect, such a program aims at renewing the faith community's appreciation for, love for, and celebration of the word of God. Without this wider and deeper emphasis, a program for readers may seem focused primarily on technical skills associated with public communication. When the announcement of the inauguration (or development) of a reader formation program is made, it should be sensed as the logical outcome of a fresh realization of the central role that the proclamation of the word plays in liturgical celebration.

Once the program has been prepared for, announced and explained in terms of a renewal in which the entire parish community is involved, it is time to invite those who want to participate in the formation and become ministers of the word. It must be clear in this invitation that certain basic skills and a considerable investment of time and effort are expected (though it shouldn't sound like a warning!) and that the potential service rendered to the assembly in this ministry is profoundly significant. The impression must be that the proclamation of the word in your community is going to take on ever-increasing significance; a promise of more gratifying and uplifting liturgical proclamation is implicit.

Discerning the necessary skills

Unless you have someone in your community who can assess basic public communication skills *and* communicate the particular adaptation of those skills to the liturgical context, it may be wise to call in a consultant for the initial assessment. The advantage of an outside consultant is simply that he or she brings a degree of objectivity and impartial judgment that may be difficult to find in your group. But such is not always the case. Regardless, the natural timidity we feel regarding critiquing another's skills must be overcome. And we all need to be cautioned against our natural tendency to take personally another's comments about our speaking ability.

Assessment is prepared for by outlining in detail what the ministry of reader will involve, both in terms of time and commitment. It should be explained that your faith community has inaugurated an intensive formation program for readers in order to enhance their celebration of the word at the liturgy. The ministry of reader requires a certain level of native ability, the willingness to develop one's skills and the readiness to participate in the new formation program. Thus, both new and experienced readers will undergo the assessment; both will profit from an ongoing critique (or review) of their skills.

The vast majority of people who come forward in response to such a call will have the basic requirements for the program: an adequate vocal instrument, self-possession, confidence, maturity, poise and sensitivity to audience diversity. But occasionally someone with great good will simply does not have what it takes to perform the ministry adequately. That person must be told that such is the case. Those whose voices are obviously too weak must be encouraged to seek another way to serve. Very young people must be encouraged to wait until at least after high school. Older men and women are probably the best group to draw from for this ministry, as long as they are physically strong enough and capable of the task. Those with disabilities should be welcomed heartily if their disability is unrelated to what the ministry will demand of them. Some disabilities are almost impossible to accommodate in the liturgical environment; others are easily accommodated. One of the finest readers I have ever heard is a former student (now a priest) who is blind. He prepares the texts in Braille and proclaims them with exceptional conviction and effectiveness.

In short, the assessment of basic skills must be forthright, honest and fair. No one is well served — neither the candidate nor the community — by an exaggerated sense of egalitarianism that could ultimately compromise the ministry.

Leadership

As we indicated earlier, the most successful formation programs tend to be led by readers themselves. In small parishes, it may be possible for one or two volunteers (or elected representatives of the group) to oversee the formation program and see it through. In larger parishes, a team may wish to divide the duties. In any case, truly dedicated and effective leadership is crucial to the success of a program that, in a sense, never ends — new readers must be formed as others retire, move out of the community or resign from the ministry for whatever reason.

The formation of beginning readers

Beginning readers should start their formation with a series of sessions concentrating on fundamental communication skills and becoming familiar with the design of the lectionary. It is quite possible that an experienced reader in the community could conduct these sessions, which can be guided with a resource book such as this one. At the same time, they should be given an introduction to the ministry of reader as it is understood by the church, and should have programmed exposure to introductory works on sacred scripture. Regular sessions should be scheduled for the purpose of giving new readers an opportunity to discuss their experience of the ministry, including both their successes and concerns.

The ongoing formation of experienced readers

Experienced readers will require, above all, the challenge of more advanced scripture study, perhaps best achieved in a regularly scheduled study group in which members share their learning according to a carefully planned schedule of assignments. But they will also require periodic review of their proclamation skills. There is no reason beginning readers cannot take part in the study and critique sessions of experienced readers. Ideally, in any community's group of readers there will be men and women at various stages of formation.

Scheduling

The most effective schedule, from the reader's point of view, will be one that provides the experience often enough to keep one's skills honed but not so often that the task becomes burdensome. However, there is room for great flexibility in the matter of scheduling. For example, it is not always best for either the reader or the assembly that a rigid linear approach be taken, that is, for each reader to be assigned, for example, once every six weeks. Some readers may find that short concentrated periods of assignment make their ministry more effective. Consider, for example, the practice of assigning the same reader to the 10:00 AM mass for every Sunday during Advent. Such an arrangement would provide the reader with the benefits of a sustained experience and the opportunity to prepare readings that are all united around the themes proper to the Advent season. The point is that readers' own preferences and the liturgical calendar may provide the best guides for effective scheduling.

Ceremonial recognition of the ministry

Once a year, on a day when the readings would make it particularly appropriate, the ministry of reader should be recognized in some ritual way during the Sunday assembly. The *Book of Blessings* contains a ceremony for the commissioning of readers. That ceremony has been reprinted here for your consideration, but you are certainly not obligated to use it. You may wish only to use it as a model for a ceremony more appropriate for your situation. A given community will know best how to devise a brief ceremony for this purpose. It is important to realize that the recognition is of the ministry and those who perform it; ultimately, such a ceremony's purpose is to remind us of the central place in our lives occupied by the proclaimed word of God. It would be quite misleading if such a ceremony gave the impression that its purpose were to thank Bob, Betty and Joe for their generosity in being readers; such gratitude is implicit when people are commissioned for a noble task. The ceremony makes it clear that their willingness to accept the ministry is another sign of the Holy Spirit at work in the church, drawing upon people's gifts and labors to ensure the spread of the good news of salvation through liturgical proclamation.

From the *Book of Blessings:*

Introduction
The word of God, as proclaimed in the sacred scripture, lies at the heart of our Christian life and is integral to all our liturgical celebrations.

This order is not intended for the institution of readers by the bishop, who uses the rite contained in the Roman Pontifical. Rather, this blessing is for parish readers who have the responsibility of proclaiming the scriptures at Mass and other liturgical services. Care should be taken to see that readers are properly prepared for the exercise of their ministry before receiving this blessing. The functions of the reader are given in no. 66 of the *General Instruction of the Roman Missal.*

If desired, each new reader may be presented with a lectionary or Bible after the prayer of blessing.

This blessing is given by the pastor, who may also delegate it to another priest or deacon.

ORDER OF BLESSING WITHIN MASS
After the gospel reading, the celebrant in the homily, based on the sacred text and pertinent to the particular place and the people involved, explains the meaning of the celebration.

General Intercessions
The general intercessions follow, either in the usual form at Mass or in the form provided here. The celebrant concludes the intercessions with the prayer of blessing. From the following intentions those best for the occasion may be used or adapted, or other intentions that apply to the particular circumstances may be composed.

The celebrant says:
The word of God calls us out of darkness into the light of faith. With the confidence of God's children let us ask the Lord to hear our prayers and to bless these readers:

R.. Lord, hear our prayer.

or:

R. Lord, graciously hear us.

Assisting minister:
For the church, that we may continue to respond to the word of God which is proclaimed in our midst, we pray to the Lord. R.

Assisting minister:
For all who listen as the scriptures are proclaimed, that God's word may find in them a fruitful field, we pray to the Lord. R.

Assisting minister:
For those who have not heard the message of Christ, that we may be willing to bring them the good news of salvation, we pray to the Lord. R.

Assisting minister:
For our readers, that with deep faith and confident voice they may announce God's saving word, we pray to the Lord. R.

Prayer of Blessing

With hands extended over the new readers the celebrant says
immediately:

Everlasting God,
when he read in the synagogue at Nazareth,
your Son proclaimed the good news of salvation
for which he would give up his life.
Bless these readers.
As they proclaim your words of life,
strengthen their faith
that they may read with conviction and boldness,
and put into practice what they read.
We ask this through Christ our Lord.
R. Amen.

[See the Book of Blessings *(Collegeville, MN: The Liturgical Press, 1989), pages*
694 – 697, for the Order of Blessing within a Celebration of the Word of God.]

11 Conclusion

One of the most significant changes in the liturgical lives of Catholic Christians has been a renewed emphasis on the Bible — the word of God. From a time not very long ago when Catholics had every right to be embarrassed about their ignorance of sacred scripture, we have come to an age in which the word of God is once again proclaimed as a heritage we can proudly claim. From a time when study of the Bible was perceived as a heady occupation for scholars only, we have come to a day when informal study groups pursue biblical literature with courage and insight. From an age when the liturgy of the church exposed us to very few of the words of sacred scripture, we have arrived at a time when the liturgical proclamation of the word once again holds it rightful place. Our Sunday assemblies come together to break open the word *and* to break the bread.

And with this resurgence of the word in our midst, it was only a matter of time before we experienced the need for ministers of that word — not just functionaries to pronounce the words aloud but true ministers called from among the people of God to become bearers of the word, lovers of the word, custodians of the word. Through their study, prayer, skills and faith, they break open the word for us. We are nourished from the lectern as well as from the altar.

Let readers accept the challenge issued them by the church's need in our day. Let them become masters of their task, lovers of their calling. Let them be John the Baptist, a herald's voice, filling in the valleys and lowering the hills, making a straight path for the Lord in the hearts of all who have ears to hear.

Critique Form for Liturgical Readers

The following critique form is an instructional tool which may be useful in the reader formation program at any stage of readers' development. It should be seen as an instructional tool, pointing out the wide range of considerations relevant to compelling ministry of the word. Whether it is used to "audition" potential readers or to encourage growth among experienced readers, it should not be seen as magic formula or the ultimate criterion for evaluation. On the other hand, it can serve as a somewhat objective (and anonymous) tool for indicating areas in which any given reader needs to improve his or her skills.

Reader: _____

Parish: _____

Verbal Considerations

Communication of Intellectual Content

5————————4————————3————————2————————1

Clearly understands   *Seems uncertain*
the meaning   *of the meaning*

Communication of Emotional Content

5————————4————————3————————2————————1

Clearly senses the mood   *Seems unaware*
and feeling   *of the mood and feeling*

Communication of Aesthetic Content

5————————4————————3————————2————————1

Clearly aware of   *Seems unaware of*
the beauty of text/content   *the beauty of text/content*

Quality of Sharing

5————————4————————3————————2————————1

Sensitive to audience,   *Seems unaware*
eager to share   *of the audience*

Vocal Projection

5————————4————————3————————2————————1

Voice fills the space   *Voice seems subdued,*
clearly, distinctly   *inadequate*

Melody

5————————4————————3————————2————————1

Wide use of vocal range,   *Monotone,*
appropriate to text   *lacks variety*

Rate

5————————4————————3————————2————————1

Varied and appropriate,   *Too fast*
energetic   *(or too slow, dull)*

Pauses

5————————4————————3————————2————————1

*Effective, enhancing
the meaning*

*Awkward, conflicting
with meaning*

Volume

5————————4————————3————————2————————1

*Appropriate for space
(easy to hear)*

*Inadequate (hard to hear)
or excessive*

Articulation

5————————4————————3————————2————————1

*Distinct, clear, easy
to understand*

*Indistinct, imprecise
(or overdone)*

Emphasis/Stress

5————————4————————3————————2————————1

*Well-placed, enhancing
the meaning*

*Ill-placed, awkward,
inconsistent with meaning*

Nonverbal Considerations

Posture

5————————4————————3————————2————————1

*Alert, strong,
yet relaxed*

*Stiff, rigid, or
too casual*

Attitude

5————————4————————3————————2————————1

*Genuine, sincere,
warm*

*Uptight, severe,
or nonchalant*

Demeanor

5————————4————————3————————2————————1

*Poised and
confident*

*Uncomfortable,
nervous, tentative*

Dress

5————————4————————3————————2————————1

*Modest, subdued,
appropriate*

*Too flashy, too casual,
or inappropriate*

Environmental Considerations

Use of Lectern and Microphone

5————————4————————3————————2————————1

*Clearly in command
of space and equipment*

*Seems unfamiliar with
space and equipment*

Liturgical Movement (procession/recessional)

5————————4————————3————————2————————1

*Poised, comfortable,
natural*

*Rigid, or too casual,
or awkward*

Additional comments: _____

_____

Pronunciation Guide

Key:

Accented syllable is marked by ″

f**a**te	**e**vil	b**i**te	h**o**pe	j**u**te
fat	bet	bit	hop	but
târ	hêr	fîr	ôr	tûrn
alas	wanted	easily	book	pull
*las	want*d	eas*ly	b*k	p*ll
sh**à**re	cow			
extr*a*	boy			

Aaron	àr″-*a*n	Archelaus	âr-ke-l**a**″-us
Abba	ab″-*a, a*-b*a*″	Arimathaea	âr-i-m*a*-th**e**″-*a*
Abel Meholah	**a**″-b*l mi-h**o**″-l*a*	Asa	**a**″-s*a*
Abiathar	*a*-b**i**″-*a*-thêr	Asher	a″-shêr
Abijah	*a*-b**i**″-j*a*	Attalia	a-t*a*-l**i**″-*a*
Abilene	a-bi-l**e**″-ne	Azariah	a-za-r**i**″-*a*
Abishai	**a**-b**i**″-sh**i**, *a*-bi″-sh**a-i**	Azor	**a**″-zôr
Abiud	*a*-b**i**″-*d		
Ahner	ab″-nêr	Baal-shalishah	ba″-*a*l-sh**a**″-li-sh*a*,
Abraham	**a**″-br*a*-ham		b**al** . . .
Abram	a″-br*a*m	Babel	b**a**″-b*l
Achaia	*a*-k**i**″-y*a, a*-k**a**″-y*a*	Babylon	ba″-bi-lon
Achim	**a**″-kim	Barabbas	bâr-ab″-*a*s
Advocate	ad″-v**o**-k**a**t	Barnabas	bâr″-na-b*a*s
Ahaz	a″-haz	Barsabbas	bâr-sa″-b*a*s
aloes	a″-l**o**z	Bartholomew	bâr-thol″-om-y**u**
Alpha	al″-f*a*	Bartimaeus	bâr-ti-m**e**″-us
Alphaeus	al-f**e**″-us	Baruch	bàr″-uk
Amalek	am″-*a*-lek	Beelzebul	b**e**-el″-z*a*-b*l
Amalekites	a-mal″-e-k**i**tz	Bethany	beth″-*a*-n**e**
Amaziah	a-m*a*-z**i**″-*a*	Bethel	beth″-el
Amminadab	a-min″-*a*-dab	Bethlehem	beth″-le-hem
Ammonites	a″-m**o**-n**i**tz	Bethphage	beth″-f*a*-je
Amon	a″-mon	Bethsaida	beth-s**a**″-i-d*a*
Amorites	a″-môr-**i**tz	Boaz	b**o**″-az
Amos	a″-mos		
Amoz	a″-moz	Caesarea	s**e**z-*a*-r**e**″-*a*
Anna	a″-n*a*	Caiaphas	k**i**″-y*a*-f*a*s, k*a*″-*a*-f*a*s
Annas	a″-n*a*s	Cana	k**a**″-n*a*
Antioch	an″-t**e**-ok	Canaan	k**a**″-n*a*n
Apollos	a-pol″-os	Canaanite	k**a**″-n*a*-n**i**t
Arabah	âr″-*a*-b*a*	Capernaum	k*-pêr″-n**a**-um
Aramaean	âr-*a*-m**e**″-*a*n	Cappadocia	ka-p*a*-d**o**″-sh*a*

Carmel	kâr-mel″	Galilean(s)	ga″-li-l**e**″-*a*n(z)
Cephas	s**e**″-f*a*s	Galilee	ga″-li-l**e**
Chaldaeans	kal-d**e**″-*a*nz	Gehazi	ge-h**a**″-z**e**, ge-h**a**″-zi
Chloe	kl**o**″-**e**	Gennesaret	ge-nes″-*a*-ret
Chronicles	kron″-i-k*lz	Gethsemane	geth-sem″-*a*-n**e**
Chuza	k**u**″-z*a*	Gibeon	gi″-b**e**-*a*n
Cilicia	s**i**-lis″-y*a*, si-lish″-a	Gilgal	gil″-gal
Cleopas	kl**e**″-**o**-p*a*s	Golgotha	gol″-g*a*-th*a*
Clopas	kl**o**″-p*a*s	Gomorrah	ge-môr″-*a*
Colossians	ko-losh″-*a*nz		
Corinth	kôr″-inth	Habakkuk	hab″-*a*-kuk
Corinthians	kôr-in″-th**e**-*a*nz		h*a*-bak″-uk
Cornelius	kôr-n**e**l″-yus	Hadad-rimmon	h**a**″-dad-rim″-on
Cretans	kr**e**″-t*a*ns	Hades	h**a**″-d**e**z
Cushite	k*sh″-**i**t	Hebron	h**e**″-bron
Cyrene	s**i**-r**e**″-ne	Hellenists	hel″-*n-ists
Cyrus	s**i**″-rus	Herodians	he-r**o**″-d**e**-*a*nz
		Hezekiah	he-ze-k**i**″-a
darnel	dâr″-nel	Hezron	hez″-ron
Damascus	d*a*-mas″-kus	Hilkiah	hil-k**i**″-*a*
Decapolis	di-ca″-po-lis	Hittite	hit″-**i**t
denarius, -rii	de-nâr″-**e**-us,	Horeb	h**o**″-reb
	de-nâr″-**e**-**e**	Hosea	h**o**-z**a**″-*a*, h**o**-z**e**″-*a*
Deuteronomy	dy**u**-t*ẽ*r-on″-o-m**e**	Hur	hûr
drachmas	drak″-m*a*z		
		Iconium	**i**-k**o**″-n**e**-um
Ebed-melech	e-bed-mel″-ek	Immanuel	i-man″-y**u**-el
Ecclesiastes	e-kl**e**-z**e**-as″-t**e**z	Isaac	**i**″-z*a*k
Elamites	el″-*a*-mitz	Isaiah	**i**-z**a**″-*a*
Eldad	el″-dad	Iscariot	is-kàr″-**e**-ot
Eleazar	el-**e**-**a**″-zèr	Israel	iz″-r*a*-el, iz″-r**e**-el
Eli	**e**″-l**i**	Israelites	iz″-r**e**-*litz″
Eli, Eli, lama	**a**″-l**e**, **a**″-l**e**, l*a*″-m*a*	Ituraea	i-t**u**-r**e**″-*a*
sabachthani	s*a*-b*a*k-t*a*″-n**e**		
Eliab	**e**-l**i**″-ab	Jairus	j**i**″-rus
Eliakim	e-l**i**″-*a*-kim	Javan	j**a**″-van
Elijah	e-l**i**″-j*a*	Jechoniah	jek-**o**-n**i**″-*a*
Elisha	e-l**i**″-sh*a*	Jehoshaphat	je-hosh″-*a*-fat,
Eliud	e-l**i**″-ud		je-hos″-*a*-fat
Eloi, Eloi, lama	**a**″-loy, **a**″-loy, l*a*″-m*a*	Jeremiah	jàr-*a*-m**i**″-*a*
sabachthani	s*a*-b*a*k-t*a*″-n**e**	Jericho	jàr″-i-k**o**
Emmanuel	e-man″-y**u**-el	Jerusalem	je-r**u**″-s*a*-lem
Emmaus	e-m**a**″-us	Jesse	jes″-**e**
Ephah	**e**″-f*a*	Jethro	jeth″-r**o**
Ephesians	e-f**e**″-zh*a*nz	Joanna	j**o**-an″-*a*
Ephphatha	ef″-*a*-th*a*	Job	j**o**b
Ephraim	**e**″-fr*a*-im, ef″-r*m	Joel	j**o**″-*l
Ephrata	**e**″-fr*a*-t*a*	Jonah	j**o**″-n*a*
Ephrathah	**e**″-fr*a*-th*a*, -t*a*	jonquil	jon″-kwil
Euphrates	y**u**-fr**a**″-t**e**z	Joram	jôr″-*a*m
Ezekiel	e-z**e**k″-**e**-el	Joses	j**o**″-ses
Ezr*a*	ez″-r*a*	Joset	j**o**″-set
		Joshua	josh″-y**u**-*a*
Gabbatha	ga″-b*a*-th*a*	Josiah	j**o**-s**i**″-*a*
Galatia	g*a*-l**a**″-sh*a*	Jotham	j**o**″-th*a*m
Galatians	g*a*-l**a**″-sh*a*nz	Judah	j**u**″-d*a*

Judaism	ju"-de-izm		Nicolaus	ni-ko-la"-us
Judas (Iscariot)	ju"-das(is-kàr"-e-ot)		Nineveh	ni"-ne-v*
Judea, judaea	ju-de"-a		Nun	nun
Justus	jus"-tus			
			Obed	o"-bed
Kedron	ked"-ron		Omega	o"-me-ga, o-me"-ga
			Onesimus	o-nes"-i-mus
Lazarus	la"-za-rus		Ophir	o"-fer
Lebanon	leb"-a-non			
Levi	le-vi		Pamphylia	pam-fi"-le-a
Levite(s)	le"-vit(z)		Parmenas	pâr"-me-nas
Leviticus	le-vit"-i-cus		Parthians	pâr"-the-anz
Libya	lib"-e-a		Patmos	pat"-mos, pat"-mos
Lud	lud		Perez	pêr"-ez
Lysanius	li-sa"-ne-us		Perga	pêr"-ga
Lystra	lis"-tra		Persia	pêr"-zha
			Phanuel	fan"-yu-el
Maccabees	mac"-a-bez		Pharaoh	fàr"-o
Macedonia	ma-sa-do"-ne-a		Pharisees	fàr"-i-sez
Magdala	mag"-da-la		Philemon	fi"-li-mon
Magdalene	mag"-da-l*n		Philippi	fi-lip"-i
Malachi	mal"-a-ki		Philippians	fi-lip"-e-anz
Malchiah	mal-ki"-a		Phrygia	fri"-je-a
Malchus	mal"-kus		phylacteries	fi-lak"-t*-rez
Mamre	mam"-re		Pisidia	pi-si"-de-a
Manasseh	ma-nas"-e		Pontius Pilate	pon"-shus pi"-l*t
manna	ma"-na		Pontus	pon"-tus
Massah	mas"-a		Portico	pôr"-ti-ko
Matthat	math"-at		Praetorium	pre-tôr"-e-um,
Matttew	math"-yu		Prochorus	pro-kôr"-us,
Matthias	ma-thi"-as			pro"-ko-rus
Medad	me"-dad		proselytes	pro"-sa-litz
Medes	medz		Put	put
Megiddo	me-gid"-o			
Melchizedek	mel-kiz"-e-dek		Qoheleth	ko-hel"-eth
Meribah	mêr"-i-ba		Quirinius	kwi-rin"-e-us
Mesopotamia	me"-so-po-ta"-me-a			
Micah	mi"-ka		Rabbuni	ra-bu"-ne
Midian	mid"-e-an		Rehab	ra"-hab
Moriah	mo-ri"-a		Ram	ram
Moshech	mo"-shek		Rehoboam	re-o-bo"-am
myrrh	mûr		Rephidim	ref"-i-dim
			Rosh	rosh, rosh
Naaman	na"-a-man		Rufus	ru"-fus
Nahshon	na"-shon			
Nain	na"-in		Sabaoth	sa"-ba-ot, sa"-ba-oth
Naphtali	naf"-ta-li		Sadduccees	sad"-ju-sez
Nathan	na"-than		Salem	sa"-lem
Nathanael	na-than"-y*l		Salmon	sal"-mon
Nazara	na"-za-ra		Salome	sa-lo"-me
Nazarene	na"-za-ren		Samaria	sa-màr"-e-a
Nazareth	na"-za-reth		Samaritian(s)	sa-màr"-i-tan(z)
Nebuchadnezzar	neb"-yu-kad-nez"-êr		Sanhedrin	san"-hi-drin,
Nehemiah	ne-he-mi"-a			san-he"-drin
Nicanor	ni-ka"-nôr		Saul	sol
Nicodemus	ni-ko-de"-mus		Scythian	sith"-e-an

Seba	se″-ba
Shaphat	sha″-fat
Sharon	shàr″-*n
Shealtiel	she-al″-te-el
Sheba	she″-ba
Shebna	sheb″-na
Shechem	she″-kem, shek″-am
Sheol	she″-ol
Shinar	shi″-nar
Shunem	shu″-nem
Shunammitess	shu″-na-mi″-tes
Sidon	si″-d*n
Sidonian	si-do″-ne-an
Silas	Si″-las
Siloam	si-lo″-am, si-lo″-am
Silvanus	sil-va″-nus
Simeon	sim″-e-*n
Sinai	si″-ni
Sion	si″-*n, zi″-*n
Sirach	si″-rak
Sodom	sod″-*m
Solomon	sol″-o-m*n
Sostheńes	sos″-the-nez
Sovereignty. -ties	sov″-rin-te(z)
Susanna	su-za″-na
Sychar	si″-kâr
Syria	se″-rea
Syrian	se″-re-an
Talitha kum	ta-li″-thakum
Tamar	ta″-mâr
Tarshish	târ″-shish
Tarsus	târ″-sus
tetrarch	tet″-rârk
Thaddaeus	tha″-de-us, tha-de″-us
Theophilus	the-of″-i-lus
Thessalonians	thes″-a-lo″-ne-anz
Thessalonika	thes″-a-lo″-ne-ka
Tiberias	ti-be″-re-as
Tiberius Caesar	ti-be″-re-us se″-zêr
Timaeus	ti-me″-us
Timon	ti″-mon
Titus	ti″-tus
Trachonitis	tra″-ko-ni″-tus
Tubal	tu″-bal
Tyre	tir
Ur	ûr
Uriah	yu-ri″-a
Uzziah	*-zi″-a
wadi	wa″-de
Zacchaeus	za-ke″-us
Zadok	za″-dok
Zarephath	zàr″-a-fat
Zealot	zel″-*t
Zebedee	zeb″-i-de
Zebulon, Zebulun	zeb″-yu-lon
Zechariah	zek″-a-ri″-a
Zedekiah	zed″-a-ki″-a
Zephaniah	zef″-a-ni″-a
Zerah	ze″-ra
Zerubbabel	ze-ru″-ba-bel
Zion	zi-*n
Ziph	zif